MYSTICAL MESSAGES OF MANIFESTATIONS

Intention, Information, Imagination, Inspiration, Intuition

Letters received from World Spiritual, Political, Business
and Economic Leaders from 1993 to 2024

DR. C.V. RAVINDRANATH

HMCT, PDSHM, MA, MPhil, PhD (Mgmt), PhD (Philo), D. Litt (SQ).

ISBN 979-8-89363-928-5

Hawa Mahal, Jaipur

Dear C V Ravindranath.

Wish you a very Happy Birthday.
May this year bring more
happiness and success in your life!

Narendra Modi

ॐ MAHA TRIPURA SUNDARIYE NAMAH:

SRI ADI SHANKARACHARYA

CURRICULUM VITAE

DR. C. V. Ravindranath

HMCT, PDSHM, MA, MPhil, PhD (Mgmt), PhD (Philo), D. Litt (SQ).

Vision and Mission Statement of DR. C. V. Ravindranath

VISION:	–	PURITY	* CREATIVITY*	SPIRITUALITY
MISSION:	–	WISDOM	* WELLNESS*	WEALTH
		(SARASWATI)	(PARVATI)	(LAXMI)

I Birth

C. V. Ravindranath was born in Colombo to an affluent family of Jewellers, ISLAND GOLD HOUSE, which was that time recognized by Her Majesty Queen Elizabeth of England. He is a Virgoan born on 24th August, 1954 at 9pm – Punnartham Nakshthram (VIRGO); in Ratna Hospital, Colombo, Ceylon.

II Alumni

1. St. Teresa's Anglo-Indian Convent – Kindergarten (Baby class) – 1960.

2. St. Michael's Anglo-Indian Boys' High School, Kannur- Anglo-Indian Schools Examination, Chennai (1961-1971) Madras Board of Anglo-Indian Examinations.

3. P.S.G College of Technology, Coimbatore – Pre-Technical (1972-1973).

4. Birla Institute of Technology and Science (BITS) Pilani, Rajasthan – 1st B Tech (Hons) - (1973-1974) (Discontinued due to extreme cold climate).

5. Institute of Hotel Management, Catering Technology and Applied Nutrition, Mumbai- HMCT, PDSHM (1976-1980).

6. Cornell University, School of Hotel Administration, USA – Hotel Sales & Marketing (1983).

7. Gemological Institute of America (GIA), USA – Fine Jewellery Sales Consultant (1991).

8. Indian Diamond Institute (IDI), Surat – Diamond – Sales (1992).

9. Indian Institute of Management (IIM), Ahmedabad – SMEP (2000).

10. Indian Institute of Kozhikode, MDP (2001).

11. Regional Engineering College & Management studies – MDP (2002).

12. Madurai Kamaraj University, Madurai – MA & MPhil (2004-2006).

13. Indian School of Business – (ISB) Hyderabad – MDP (2007).

14. Kannur University, Dept. of Philosophy, PhD – The Prospects of Meditative Techniques in Transforming Socio – Personal Domains of Fundamentalism (2008-2013).

15. International Open University, Colombo, Honorary PhD in SQ in Business Management (2014).

16. Academy for Spiritual Scientist – Kingship Academy: Honorary Doctorate in Spirituality (2015).

Disclaimer

Source Links and Image Copyright Information

I extend my heartfelt gratitude to the websites that have generously allowed me to incorporate their images in this book. These captivating visuals have undoubtedly enhanced the reader's experience and added depth to the content.

I would like to acknowledge the hard work and creativity of the website owners and contributors who have curated and produced these remarkable images. Without their dedication, this book would not have been as visually engaging.

- Shri KR Narayanan: Ratna Sagar Rajkamal, CC BY-SA, via Wikimedia Commons
- Swami Tejomayananda via www.chinmayamission.com
- Narendra Modi, CC BY-SA 2.0, via Wikimedia Commons

CONTENTS

PREFACE

The book entitled **"Mystical Messages of Manifestations"** is a collection of emails and letters received from eminent dignitaries from all walks of life and is an acknowledgement to **DR. C. V. Ravindranath Ji** for his contribution in the field of education, business and spirituality. The appreciation expressed in every letter/e.mail is an apt illustration of his ardent fervour in all his undertakings. Such enthusiasm in fulfilling one's heart's desire should not be overlooked. Hence the recognition he has obtained through the innumerable messages given in the book "MYSTICAL MESSAGES OF MANIFESTATIONS" is justified. He deserves a lot more applause for his perseverance, one pointed dedication, diligent concern and the humane approach that he has adopted in all his noble ventures for the benefit of the society.

The very title **"MYSTICAL MESSAGES OF MANIFESTATIONS"** itself is an ample proof to make us aware of his innate and perpetual oneness with the All Pervasive Unseen Power – Adi Parashakti. He has always been immersed in Maha Meru Sree Vidyopasna, which has made him realize that the entire universe is a manifestation of DEVI Herself and the messages received are Her Mystical Reverberations.

Dr. C. V. Ravindranath Ji is a pure soul dedicated to the Oneness of SHIVA - SHAKTI and is well aware that Shakti is the manifestation of SHIVA, the Unchanging immortal, ever pervading Consciousness, which is Truth Itself. This book is sure to inspire readers in all fields of activity, be they be materially or spiritually inclined. All his works, for e.g. The Beauty of Intuitive Creativity, Trinity So Divine exhort the readers that Sree Vidyopasna should be an integral part of one's life to preserve and sustain wealth, wellness and wisdom. An excellent academic scholar and a successful business man, he has always given due attention to spiritual teachings thus proving himself to be a Karmayogi, a Bhakta and a Jnana Yogi at the same time.

All his ventures are assets to his fellow beings. May Dr. Ravindranath Ji soar greater heights in all his endeavours. Blessed is, Dr. Ravindranath Ji with the grace of The All Pervading Power.

With Best Wishes in the Absolute Truth,   **15.4.2024**

Swamini Devi Jnanabha Nishtananda Giri

Santhananda Mutt

Rishi Jnana Sadhanalayam

Pathanamthitta, Kerala

FOREWORD

"Mystical Messages of Manifestations" consists of Letters of Hopes by our esteemed author's mission and vision for societal betterment through dialogue and collaboration with World Spiritual, Political, Business and Economic leaders from 1993 to 2024. This book elaborates on five I's Intention, Information, Imagination, Inspiration, Intuition by the author for Progress and prosperity of the world.

The first Chapter Universalism consists of letters of great hopes for World Peace from the global leaders of our times from Shri Narendra Modi, Honourable Prime Minister of India, Mr. Joe Biden, Honorable President of the United States of America, Office of Prime Minister of Israel, Mr. Benjamin Netanyahu, Shri Shashi Tharoor, Member of Lok Sabha, Mr. Bill Clinton, Former President of United States of America etc.

Chapter 2 -Divine Blessings from the World Spiritual leaders like His Holiness Gurudev Swami Chinmayanandaji, His Holiness Swami Tejomayananda ji, The Holy Father from the Vatican and other Gurus who has transcended his consciousness to the highest realms of knowledge.

Health is Wealth- Chapter 4 consists of advices from Great people in the field of Medical Care and Support like Ministry of Ayush, Govt of India, Dr. Jill Bolte Talyor, Author of My stroke of Insight and Whole Brain Living, Time 100 Most Influential which had helped him to strive after Ramsay Hunt Syndrome and brain stroke in 2016.

In the Chapter IV – Positivity in Business – The author gets inspiration and motivation from great scholars of his times that include letters from Shri. Rajeev P, Scientist and Head, Bureau of Indian Standards, Shri. Ratan Tata, Former Chairman, Tata Sons Limited, Shri Narayan Murthy, Chairman, Infosys, Capt. C P Krishnan Nair, Chairman, Hotel Leela Venture Limited, Mr. Wayne Gilcrease, Gemological Institute of America etc. This inspired him to do business with Zeal and positive energy, promoting IQ, and EQ in business Management.

In the last chapter, Economic Growth consists of letters of hope for the Economic Growth of India from 12-6-1972 to 6.11.2023. This depicts the authors strive to create wealth for our mother country for the welfare of our citizens of the Mother Land. His vision for Economic growth of Kannur manifested to bring Kannur International Airport, Development of Payambalam beach etc.

The letters portray his vigorous efforts to bring Kannur on a Global platform. The ideologies from the Great World Leaders, His Role Models, Mentors and Gurus shaped him to become India's first BIS Certified Jeweller – The Torch Bearer of Gold Purity in India at Krishna Jewels, Kannur, Kerala and also to create Krishna Beach Resort, World's First Resort built on Tantric Vaastu Shilpa Shastra at Kannur, Kerala, India.

Sanita Ravindranath Cheleri　　　　　　　　　　　　　　　　　　　**17.4.2024**
BHM, MBA (USA)

CHAPTER I

UNIVERSALISM

Global Leaders can help us to develop our perception and Awareness regarding Universal Compassion and friendship for Peace Making and Peace Keeping.

There are 17 letters of great hopes for World peace from the global leaders of our times.

प्रधान मंत्री
Prime Minister

New Delhi
माघ 05, शक संवत् 1944
25th January, 2023

Dr. C V Ravindranath Ji,

Gratitude for your warm wishes for the year 2023. Greetings to you and your family on the occasion. The constant affection of our countrymen fills me with fresh energy and inspires me to continue striving for the nation's progress.

As is said, 'परिमितं भूतम् अपरिमितं भव्यम्।' meaning the past is limited, while the future is unlimited. Learning from the memories and challenges of the past year, we have to march forward continuously and work together for the nation's progress.

Amrit Kaal is 'Kartavya Kaal' for all of us to us to work wholeheartedly to fulfil the lofty resolve of building a self-reliant and glorious India. I am confident that with the spirit of 'Nation First, Always First', your efforts will ensure the progress of our nation and the society.

I pray that may 2023 become an unforgettable year of positive changes, attaining goals and success. I once again extend my greetings to you and your family on the occasion.

With best wishes for good health and a bright future.

Yours,

(Narendra Modi)

Dr. C V Ravindranath
Krishna Jewels, Jawahar Road
Thavakkara, Kannur
Kerala-670001

प्रधान मंत्री
Prime Minister

New Delhi
आश्विन 15, शक संवत् 1944
07th October, 2022

Dr. C. V. Ravindranath Ji,

I deeply value and appreciate the birthday greetings and warm wishes expressed through your letter. Your caring and affectionate thoughts have filled me with fresh energy and vigour to keep striving in service of the nation.

The Amrit Kaal of the next 25 years leading to a century of our independence is an opportunity to realise the vision of building a strong and glorious New India. Through a collective approach and Jan Bhagidari, let us aim bring about an unprecedented positive transformation.

I thank you once again for the thoughtful gesture. Best wishes for your sustained good health and well-being.

Warm regards,

Yours,

(Narendra Modi)

Dr. C. V. Ravindranath
Krishna Jewels
Kannur
Kerala- 670001

प्रधान मंत्री
Prime Minister

New Delhi
कार्तिक 13, शक संवत् 1944
4th November, 2022

Dr. C. V. Ravindranath Ji,

Heartfelt gratitude to you for Deepavali greetings. Many wishes to you and your family for the festival of lights. May this auspicious festival bring new energy and enthusiasm in our lives.

सर्वज्ञे सर्ववरदे सर्वदुष्टभयंकरि ।
सर्वदुःखहरे देवि महालक्ष्मि नमोऽस्तुते॥

Deepavali is a symbol of victory of light over darkness, good over evil and knowledge over ignorance. May we imbibe its spirit and become a medium of bringing happiness and positive changes in the lives of others.

The journey towards 100 years of independence by the year 2047 is a golden period for building a strong, self-reliant nation. I am sure that a nation energised by the collective resolve of the countrymen will scale new heights of progress during the Amrit Kaal.

I pray to Maa Lakshmi for your happiness, prosperity and well-being. Greetings once again for Deepavali.

Yours,

(Narendra Modi)

Dr. C. V. Ravindranath
Jawahar Road, Thavakkara
Kannur
Kerala- 670001

अत्यमेव जयते

प्रधान मंत्री
Prime Minister

Panch Praan
for a
Prosperous India

The period of the next 25 years is the Amrit
Kaal leading up to a century of independence.
Let us make it a defining era in the history of
our country. To do so, let us embrace the
'Panch Praan', five principles that will take
India to greater heights.

Goal of Developed India - Viksit Bharat

Remove any trace of colonial mindset

Celebrate our heritage

Strengthen unity

Focus on duties

THE WHITE HOUSE
WASHINGTON

January 10, 2022

Dear Dr. CVR,

Thank you for taking the time to share your thoughts with me. Hearing from passionate individuals like you inspires me every day, and I welcome the opportunity to respond to your letter.

Our country faces many challenges, and the road we will travel together will be one of the most difficult in our history. Despite these tough times, I have never been more optimistic for the future of America. I believe we are better positioned than any country in the world to lead in the 21st century not just by the example of our power but by the power of our example.

While we may not always agree on how to solve every issue, I pledge to be a President for all Americans. I am confident that we can work together to find common ground to make America a more just, prosperous, and secure Nation.

As we move forward to address the complex issues of our time, I encourage you to remain an active participant in helping write the next great chapter of the American story. We need your courage and dedication at this critical time, and we must meet this moment together as the United States of America. If we do that, I believe that our best days still lie ahead.

Sincerely,

THE WHITE HOUSE
WASHINGTON

Gmail - FW: Response to Your Message
December 1, 2021

Dear Dr. Ravindranath,

Thank you for writing to me about U.S. foreign policy. I appreciate the time you took to write, and I welcome the opportunity to respond.

The challenges facing our world today demonstrate how interconnected we are and how the fates of all people are bound up together. The outbreak of a virus overseas can cause profound grief and suffering at home. Conflict a continent away can create unrest that endangers our own security. Economic downturns abroad can mean lost jobs and shuttered businesses in towns across America. Global climate change is already worsening hurricanes in the Gulf, floods in the heartland, and wildfires in the West. No country can solve these problems alone, and America cannot afford to be absent from the world stage. Investing in strengthening our leadership abroad is also an investment in bolstering our security and prosperity at home.

As President, I am determined to repair our alliances, renew our leadership in international institutions, reclaim our credibility, and equip the American middle class to succeed in a global economy. I strongly believe that our Nation is better positioned than any other to lead in the 21st century and to be the greatest force for good in the world. Under my Administration, American political and economic leadership will be rooted in our most cherished values: defending freedom, championing opportunity, upholding universal rights, respecting the rule of law, and treating every person with dignity.

We have returned diplomacy to the center of our foreign policy and are committed to meeting today's global challenges from a position of strength, working in close cooperation with our allies and partners. I also want to be clear that I will never hesitate to defend the American people or our vital interests, including through the use of force when necessary. We will always stand with our friends around the world to protect our values and to advance peace, security, and prosperity for all.

I appreciate you sharing your views with me, and I will keep your perspective on these important issues in mind as we work to meet the challenges of our time. May God bless America, and may God protect our troops, our diplomats, our development experts, and all those serving in harm's way.

Sincerely,

לשכת ראש הממשלה

Prime Minister's Bureau

August 23, 2011

כ״ג אב, תשע״א

Mr. C.V. Ravindranath
Kunhikannan Jewellery Gold House
Kannur 670 001
Kerala
India

Dear Mr. Ravindranath,

We thank you for the two books of poetry which you sent to Prime Minister Benjamin Netanyahu, and appreciate the kind gesture.

We hope that your complaint has been resolved to your satisfaction.

Sincerely,

Rivka Kidron
Adviser to the Prime Minister

רח׳ קפלן 3, הקריה, ירושלים מיקוד 91919 טל: 02-6705555, פקס: 02-5664838

3 Kaplan St. Hakirya, Jerusalem 91919, Israel Tel: 972-2-6705555, Fax: 972-2-5664838

Prime Minister's Office

המטה לביטחון לאומי
National Security Council

משרד ראש הממשלה

May 30, 2011
כ״ו אייר תשע״א

Mr. C.V. Ravindranath
Kunhikannan Jewellery Gold House
Kannur 670 001
Kerala
India

Dear Mr. Ravindranath,

On behalf of Prime Minister Benjamin Netanyahu, we acknowledge receipt of your letter dated May 5, 2011, the contents of which have been noted.

We were sorry to learn of the inconvenience you suffered, and have forwarded your letter to the relevant department at the Israeli Ministry of Foreign Affairs for their attention and consideration.

Sincerely,

Eitan Naeh
Senior Director
Diplomatic Secretariat

c.c.   Mr. Haim Hoshen, Director
Southeast Asia Dept., Ministry of Foreign Affairs

United Nations ✹ Nations Unies

HEADQUARTERS · SIEGE   NEW YORK, NY 10017

TEL.: 1 (212) 963.2912 · FAX: 1 (212) 963.4361

3 January 2007

Dear Mr. Ravindranath,

Thank you for sharing your Ph.D. thesis on meditation and yoga with me. Quieting of mind and body is certainly needed in today's hectic world, and all healing practices can provide substantial benefit.

With best wishes for the further pursuit of your goals.

Yours sincerely,

Shashi Tharoor
Under-Secretary-General
for Communications and Public Information

Mr. C.V. Ravindranath
Kunhikannan Jewellery Gold House
Kannur – 670 001, Kerala
India

Thank you so much for your kind gift. I appreciate your thoughtfulness and generosity. You have my best wishes.

Bill Clinton

BILL CLINTON - USA

**PRÉSIDENCE
DE LA
RÉPUBLIQUE**

Le Chef de Cabinet

SCP/CdO/L065083

Paris, le   **2 7 JUIL. 1999**

Cher Monsieur,

Le Président de la République française m'a confié le soin de répondre à votre lettre.

Croyez bien que le Chef de l'Etat apprécie le souci d'information et d'échange dont votre correspondance porte témoignage.

Monsieur Jacques CHIRAC demeure ouvert au dialogue avec tous ceux qui veulent bien lui faire part de leurs attentes et de leurs propositions.

A cet égard, je puis vous assurer que votre analyse a fait l'objet d'un examen attentif.

Veuillez agréer, Chère Monsieur, l'expression de mes sentiments les meilleurs.

Annie LHERITIER

Monsieur C.V. RAVINDRANATH
Kunhikannan Jewellery
Gold House
KANNUR - 670 001
Kerala
INDE

Office of the
Prime Minister

Cabinet du
Premier ministre

Ottawa, Canada K1A 0A2

July 8, 1999

C.V. Ravindranath
Kunikannan Jewellery Gold House
Kannur - 670 001
Kerala
INDIA

Dear C.V. Ravindranath:

On behalf of the Right Honourable Jean Chrétien, I would like to acknowledge receipt of your correspondence of June 15 regarding world security.

You may be assured that your comments have been carefully reviewed. A copy of your correspondence has been forwarded to the Honourable Lloyd Axworthy, Minister of Foreign Affairs. I am certain that the Minister will appreciate being made aware of your views and will want to give them every consideration.

Yours sincerely,

R. S. Weber
Executive Correspondence Officer

Canada

2000

Minister of Foreign Affairs   Ministre des Affaires étrangères

Ottawa, Canada K1A 0G2

SEP 2 0 1999

C. V. Ravindranath
Managing Partner
Kunhikannan Jewellery
Gold House
Kannur - 670 001
Kerala
India

Dear C. V. Ravindranath:

Thank you for your letter of June 15, 1999, concerning international terrorism. The Prime Minister has also forwarded to me a copy of your correspondence about this matter. I have noted your comments about Islamic fundamentalism and regret that a heavy volume of mail has prevented me from replying as soon as I would have liked.

Canada has long taken a forceful stand, consistent with international standards of human rights, in the fight against terrorism. We have developed policies and laws that are based on the objective that terrorism must be prevented, that all perpetrators of terrorist acts must be brought to swift justice, and that terrorists should be denied sanctuary and support.

The Canadian government is convinced that combatting terrorism requires international cooperation and coordination. Canada has worked with the Economic Summit (G-8) countries for over twenty years in combatting terrorism. Initiatives taken by the Economic Summit have dealt with issues such as hijacking, hostage taking and support for terrorism. We have signed all eleven – and ratified all but one – of the international conventions to counter specific terrorism activities. These conventions counter crimes such as hijacking, theft of nuclear material and hostage taking. Canada also works within the United Nations to promote the implementation of measures to eliminate international terrorism.

- 2 -

In 1995, Canada hosted a Ministerial meeting on terrorism which was attended by representatives of all the G-8 nations as well as the European Union Presidency. The Ottawa Declaration on Counter-Terrorism, a comprehensive document spelling out what should be done globally to fight terrorism, was approved at this meeting.

In line with the Ottawa Declaration, Canada is actively participating in international meetings in order to further the objectives of the Guidelines for Action approved by the Ottawa Ministerial meeting. If you have access to the Internet and wish to learn more about the Department of Foreign Affairs and International Trade's policies and programs, you may visit our web site at the following address: **http://www.dfait-maeci.gc.ca**.

Thank you for writing to express your concerns.

Sincerely,

Lloyd Axworthy

Office of the   Cabinet du
Prime Minister   Premier ministre

Ottawa, Canada K1A 0A2

September 22, 1998

C.V. Ravindranath,
Kunikannan Jewellery Gold House,
Kannur - 670 001,
Kerala,
INDIA

Dear C.V. Ravindranath:

On behalf of the Right Honourable Jean Chrétien, I would like to acknowledge receipt of your correspondence.

You may be assured that your comments have been carefully reviewed. A copy of your correspondence has been forwarded to the Honourable Lloyd Axworthy, Minister of Foreign Affairs. I am certain that the Minister will appreciate being made aware of your views and will want to give them every consideration.

Yours sincerely,

Robert S. Weber
Special Assistant
Correspondence

Canadä

UNITED NATIONS  NATIONS UNIES

POSTAL ADDRESS—ADRESSE POSTALE: UNITED NATIONS, N.Y. 10017
CABLE ADDRESS—ADRESSE TELEGRAPHIQUE: UNATIONS NEWYORK

30 November 1998

Dear Mr. Ravindranath,

This is to acknowledge receipt of your letter of 27 October 1998.

In response to your concern, I would like to inform you that the problem of international terrorism has been on the agenda of the General Assembly of the United Nations from 1972. Some eleven international instruments have since been adopted under the auspices of both the United Nations and its specialized agencies to foster international cooperation in combating specific terrorist activities. In 1996, the General Assembly established an Ad Hoc Committee to address in depth the issue of the international legal framework for the fight against terrorism. The Convention on the Suppression of Terrorist Bombing was adopted in 1997 and some 36 countries have already signed the instrument. The Center for International Crime Prevention of the United Nations Secretariat, located in Vienna, is also taking measures to enhance international cooperation and improve the response of Governments to terrorism in all its forms and manifestations.

I trust you will find this information of interest.

Sincerely yours,

Roy S. Lee
Director
Codification Division
Office of Legal Affairs

M. C.V. Ravindranath
Managing Partner
Kunhikannan Jewellery
Gold House
Kannur - 670 001

Foreign &
Commonwealth
Office

London SW1A 2AH

Telephone: 0171

03 November 1998

C V Ravindranath
Kunhikannan Jewellery Gold House
Kannur 670 001
Kerale
India

Dear Mr Ravindranath

Thank you for your letter of 24 August to the Prime Minister about the US strikes against targets in Afghanistan and Sudan. I have been asked to reply. This year we have seen horrifying attacks against civilians in Nairobi and Dar es Salaam, Omagh and Cape Town. These incidents have highlighted the fact that terrorism can strike anywhere indiscriminately and that the majority of victims are ordinary people.

The Prime Minister issued his statement following the strikes to make clear publicly that we stand resolutely against terrorism. It is imperative that those people who might contemplate terrorism around the world understand that they cannot act with impunity.

The UK has perhaps suffered more than most countries at the hands of terrorists in recent years and we have seen the terrible devastation the terrorist's bomb can bring to our communities and people. The new Criminal Justice (Terrorism and Conspiracy) Act will provide vital help to our authorities in their fight against terrorism.

Yours sincerely

R. Dunning

Raymond Dunning
Counter Terrorism Policy Department

PRÉSIDENCE
DE LA
RÉPUBLIQUE

Le Chef de Cabinet

SCP/CdO/L065083

Paris, le   2 1 OCT. 1998

Cher Monsieur,

      Le Président de la République française m'a confié le soin de répondre à votre lettre.

      Je puis vous assurer qu'il a été pris connaissance de vos réflexions avec toute l'attention requise.

      En vous priant d'excuser le retard avec lequel vous recevez ce courrier, veuillez agréer, Cher Monsieur, l'expression de mes sentiments les meilleurs.

Annie LHERITIER

Monsieur C.V. RAVINDRANATH
Kunhikannan Jewellery Gold House
KANNUR - 670 001
KERALA
INDE

CHAPTER II

DIVINE BLESSINGS!

I am very grateful to His Holiness Gurudev Chinmayananda Swamiji for enkindling my Spiritualism with Divine Blessings.

We have here 29 divine letters from Gurus and Spiritual Leaders to transcend my consciousness to the highest realms of knowledge. Nothing purifies like knowledge.

Letters from 30.4.1990 to 23.1.2023 for enlightenment of my mind and soul.

Great minds discuss ideas. Medium minds discuss events. Small minds discuss people.

1/23/23, 2:48 PM   Gmail - My Stroke of Insight review

 Gmail   Ravindranath C.V <sudhacvr@gmail.com>

My Stroke of Insight review

Swamini Jnanabhanishta <swjn123@gmail.com>   Mon, Jan 23, 2023 at 2:28 PM
To: "Ravindranath C.V" <sudhacvr@gmail.com>

Namaste Dear Dr. Ravindranath Sir,

Hope you are keeping fine.

The preface, for "MY STROKE OF INSIGHT" by DR. JILL BOLTE TAYLOR, PhD, written by you is an apt illustration of your divinity.
Thank you very much for sending me the preface, so I got an opportunity to go through the said book. You have been chosen as a Son of Lalitha Parameswari to propagate the eternal truth through all your profound and noble deeds.
My heartfelt prayers and best wishes will be there with you and your family.
May you be blessed by Adi Parashakti in each and every moment forever.

Looking forward to meet you all on International Women's Day

With Prayers and Gratitude.

DEVI JNANABHA NISHTA.
SANTHANANDA MUTT RISHI JNANA SADHANALAYAM
SREE SANTHANANDA VIDYA NIKETHAN.
PATHANAMTHITTA ,KERALA
E-MAIL: swjn123@gmail.com
MOBILE:**9061138520.**

cv Ravindranth

From:	anna-katharina Leuthold [annakatharinaleuthold@gmail.com]
Sent:	Sunday, October 30, 2022 2:50 AM
To:	cv Ravindranth
Subject:	Fwd: Tantric Numerology of Madam Anna Katharina
Attachments:	image.png; ATT00066.htm; Tantric Numerology of Madam Anna Katharina.docx; ATT00069.htm

Sent from my iPhone

Begin forwarded message:

From: anna-katharina Leuthold <annakatharinaleuthold@gmail.com>
Date: 29 October 2022 at 11:55:46 GMT+5:30
To: reservations@kbrkannur.com
Subject: Re: Tantric Numerology of Madam Anna Katharina

Respected Dr. Ravindranath
Seeing on the photo that i was not holding the light not with both hands so sorry!!! Reding your book not finished jet (slow reading) i am still working getting 100% nature's will!!! For me it truly means to live Vegan. Not easy in India for me. Never i meet such a Spirituell Person like you in this world!!! I would love to stay in your wonderful creation for ever!!! Thank you ▢ so much for you healing techniques energies and your wonderful staff and creative place so beautiful!!! Everyone was taking care for me!!! In perfekt health i leave this place on Monday morning. Knowing that i will come back make's it easy! I wish you the highest and permanent!!!▢ Best Regards Anna
Sent from my iPhone

On 27 Oct 2022, at 08:43, anna-katharina Leuthold <annakatharinaleuthold@gmail.com> wrote:

Sent from my iPhone

Begin forwarded message:

From: anna-katharina Leuthold
<annakatharinaleuthold@gmail.com>
Date: 21 October 2022 at 20:08:33 GMT+5:30
To: cv Ravindranth <sudhacvr@gmail.com>
Subject: Re: Tantric Numerology of Madam Anna Katharina

Dear DR. Ravindranath
▢Thank you Thank you Thank you▢ for taking so much time for me! It is all so accurate! Now i have a lot work to do. To integrate all the negative aspects. Looking forward for my new Routine easy with all your wonderful Techniques! Did 5 o clock Mudras very effective!!! Feeling already so much better! Thankfully ▢ ▢ ▢ Anna

1

There sat on seashore a man of the sea.

Glazing in horizons of blue intrigue.
A jeweller looking into the golden sunsets.
There was the world and it's people, it's drama and its ways, a thousand connects, and yet his soul belonged to the sea, to its waves, to its shades, to it's moods, it's seasons and its depths, a depth which hid its deep ageless secrets.

He sat on, mesmerized by the lady of the sea, as life went by throwing many shades of emotions, on his face, in his moist eyes and on his heartbeats. Its winds dried his tears, touched and healed his wounds, scars of worldly existence, it held him, whispering healing into his heart. In its agelessness was a promise to take him away into her, within her and forever into their oneness.

There he still sits waiting.... The man of the seas.

Ramith Jayarajan

Narayanashrama
Tapovanam

Ref. No. 26640201902/2022   7th February 2019

Dear and blessed Ravindranath :

Harih Om Tat Sat. I have your letter of 7th Jan and the Tantric Management book before me. I glanced through the book, after reading your letter. It is well prepared.

Apparently, you have struck a new spiritual dimension in professional and industrial life, where spirituality seems to be the undeniable nucleus, centre, and all the rest revolving around it. In fact, is this not the way the entire world, the creation itself, is?

In our own being, besides the material body, consisting of matter and energy, is the inner triplet of mind, intelligence and ego, all functional notes of the one distinct presence, nay splendour called Consciousness. Consciousness is indefinable. Yet we can denote it as that presence which has the potential to reveal the others as well as itself. That is how we feel and say 'I am', and 'I have a body'. This expresses itself as the three distinct states of wakefulness, dream and sleep. In sleep everything else including the body and the world stands obliterated. I alone shines, but making us know that only when we wake up.

We cannot say 'we are sleeping', as we say 'we are wakeful'. Sleep is the state of the singular unalloyed subject, whereas wakefulness and dream are allied with objects.

If and when one is able to feel and say 'I am sleeping', the entire mystery of life and creation will have been ripped open – as the great, but brief, Mandukya Upanishad in its 7th mantra proclaims. You must have already reflected, I feel, on this and allied points of revelation.

For any human in any field of activity, dharma is the first and last watchword to be adhered to. Ensuring this, he can and must strive for building his resources to meet his life's needs and contribute to the society at large. In the process, he can also fulfill his legitimate desires, kaama. But none should stop with these two. Mind can hold as well as leave its possessions with mastery,

Venginissery, PO Paralam, Thrissur, 680563, Kerala, Ph 0487-2278363, Email
ashram@bhoomananda.org

which marks the real dignity and greatness of the human. Thus all the three purusharthas lead to the last, moksha, leaving all and living with one's intrinsic freedom, fullness and fulfillment.

I felt like knowing a little more about you, and sent Narayanan Nambiar, my disciple, to meet you and spend some time heartily. I think the meeting was fulfilling to both.

I am sending a set of books which you may relish. Quietitude of Mind, Science of Inner Redemption and My Beloved Baba must be interesting to you specially. Science of Inner Redemption is a unique writing on the great spiritual treatise of Yogavasishtha Ramayana, wherein Sage Vasishtha imparts the 16-year-old Sri Rama of Ayodhya the supreme secrets and revelations of the supra-sensory and supra-mental dimensions of the human personality. Rama could absorb the message and remain immersed in himself during the instruction itself. Vasishthadeva had to stop the narration for a while, and only when the prince regained normalcy, he could continue the narration. It shows how effective the message of a Knower can be on the mind and intelligence. It is a marvel indeed.

I relished what all Narayanan told me after meeting you. May be, we shall come to know each other more.

May you have all health, astuteness and dispassion to act freely, but effectively.

Love and *ashirvaad*. Swami Nirviseshananda Tirtha and Ma Gurupriya send loving good wishes.

Antaraatma,

Swami Bhoomananda Tirtha

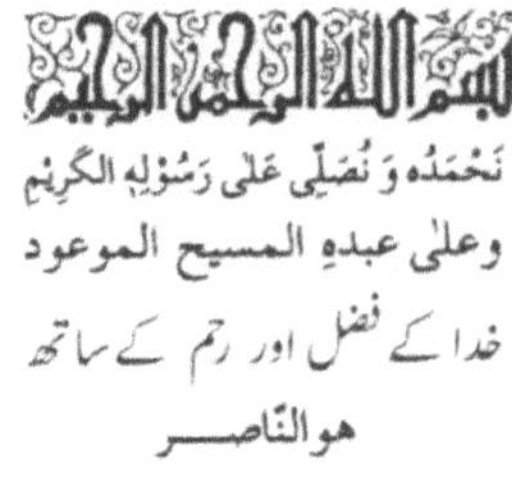

London

HM – 19-02-2018

Dear Dr. C. V. Ravindranath Sahib,

اَلسَّلَامُ عَلَیْکُمْ وَرَحْمَةُ اللهِ وَ بَرَکَاتُه

I have received your letter suggesting certain proposals and solutions for end fundamentalism and terrorism. *JazakAllah*

May Allah the Almighty bestow you with His choicest favours, make you successful in your noble objectives and may He embrace you with warmth and serenity.

May Allah be your Guide and Helper and keep you always in His special care. *Amin*

Wassalam

Yours sincerely,

MIRZA MASROOR AHMAD
Khalifatul-Masih V

India

ravindranath

From:	Swami Tejomayananda [guruji@chinmayamission.com]
Sent:	Tuesday, April 05, 2016 9:02 PM
To:	ravindranath
Subject:	Re: H.H. Swami Tejomayanda

Dear Shri Ravindranath,

Hari Om! Greetings from Singapore!

Thank you very much for your email. I am pleased and impressed to see that you and family members are becoming great scholars. Hearty Congratulations!

Noted about your love and concern for Swamini Apoorvananda.

I will speak to our Pune centre so that they can invite her more and more to Pune. I don't think any transfer is needed.

Greetings to all at home.

With Prem & Om,

Tejomayananda

On Mon, Apr 4, 2016 at 12:16 PM, ravindranath <sudhacvr@gmail.com> wrote:

UNTO HIM OUR BEST
*Pujya Gurudev, Swami Chinmayanandaji's Birth Centenary Celebrations
1916-2016*

Central Chinmaya Mission Trust
Saki Vihar Road
Mumbai 400 072
INDIA
Ph: +91-22-2857 2367
Fax: +91-22-2857 3065
www.chinmayamission.com

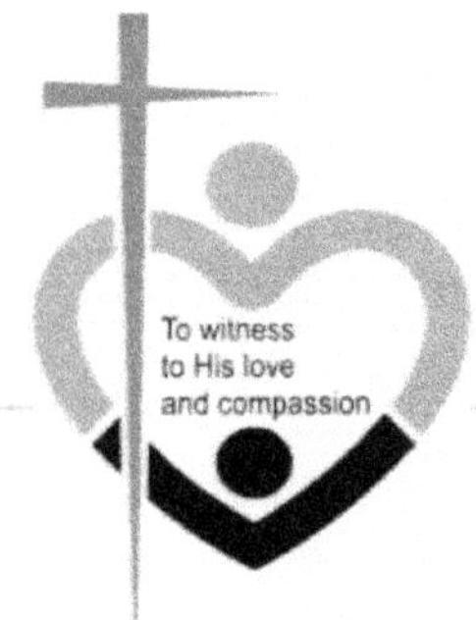

Rt. Rev. Dr. Alex Vadakumthala
Bishop of Kannur

Bishop's House, Chovva P.O., Kannur - 670 006
Tel. +91-0497-2729977, +91-0497-2729966 (P)
Mob: +91-9539918966, Fax: +91-0497-2729955
E-mail: fralexv@gmail.com, cnn_diocese@sancharnet.in
www.kannurdiocese.com

Date: 17.05.2014

Mr. C.V. Ravindranath HMCT, PDSHM, MA, MPhil
Fine Jewellery Sales Consultant (Hons.) GIA-USA
Managing Partner
Krishna Jewels
Thavakkara, Kannur.

Dear Mr Ravindranath,

I was in receipt of your letter wishing me for this new appointment in Kannur. Though it is delayed to reply to you I value greatly your kind gesture and I extend my sincere gratitude for your greetings on my Episcopal Ordination. May the blessings of the Lord be with you and grant you health, happiness and prosperity throughout your life.

Yours sincerely,

+Alex Vadakumthala
Bishop of Kannur

From the Vatican, 4 December 2008

Dear Mr. Ravindranath,

The Holy Father wishes me to express his gratitude for your kind letter and gifts. He appreciates your thoughtful gesture.

His Holiness will remember you in his prayers. He invokes upon you God's blessings of joy and peace.

Yours sincerely,

Monsignor Gabriele Caccia
Assessor

Mr. C. V. Ravindranath
Kunhikannan Jewellery Gold House
Kannur   670011
Kerala

Hari Om

Swamini Apoorvananda Saraswathi

CHINMAYA BALA BHAVAN, KANNUR - 670 001, KERALA

Balabhavan : 0497- 2700876
Vidyalaya : 2769633
College : 2706659
Resi : 2712626
E-mail : cnn_chinbala@sancharnet.in

24th May '10

Blessed dear Ravindranji
Hari Om! Salutation!
May His Grace And Blessings
Flow through us to the world around us.
Thank you very much for your
divine help. I never ever forget this kind Service
you have done to me. Because to see my
Guruji is the most important thing in
my life. Really Speaking I was living in
the waves of difficulties.
Suddenly you came as a
'GOD FATHER' and helped me. Thanks a lot my dear.
In the Service of the Lord
Swami Apoorvananda

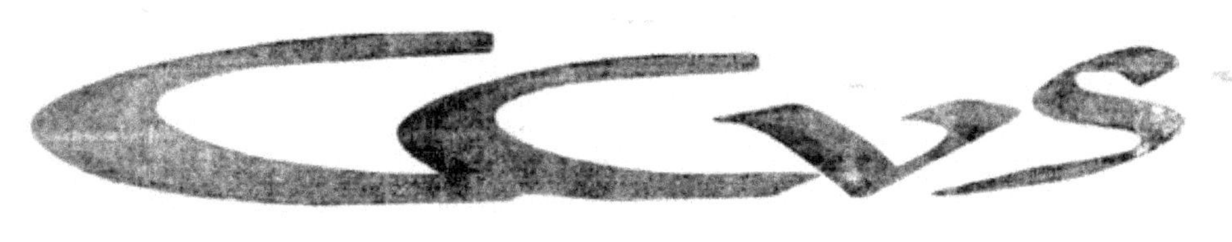

CENTRAL CHINMAYA VANPRASTH SANSTHAN
A Wing of Central Chinmaya Mission Trust For Senior Citizens.

RASOOLABAD GHAT ROAD, ALLAHABAD-211004 (INDIA)

Phones : 546602, 546541
Fax   : 0532-640078
          0532-607066

H. H. Swami Tejomayananda
Chairman

Camp: Kannur
Date.. 8th MAY, 2004

Shri Ravindranathji
The Krishna Beach,
Kannur - 67000s

Blessed Shri Ravindranathji
Hari Om, Hari Om,

We are indeed very grateful to you for the beautiful accomodation provided to us for the 4 days of cvs Camp. We are particularly appreciative of the consideration and courtesy extended to us by your beloved wife Smt Sudhaji and our Beti Sulcha.

Apart from other factors our Camp in Kannur will ever remain in our memory for the blessings received by us from your immortal neighbour, the ever active ocean.

With Blessings and Om,

Thyself in the Service of the Lord
SHIV SWARUP
Secy. Genl. ccvs.

Our thanks are equally due to our elder daughters Sunita & Sarita

8.5.04

| Reply | Reply to All | Forward | Delete | Previous | Next | Compose New | Inbox | Logout |

From	"Sumati Chaitanya" <hariomcirs@eth.net>
To	"Ravi-Sudha" <cvravi@bgl.vsnl.net.in>
Cc	
Subject	hari om
Date	Fri, 20 Dec 2002 18:04:15 +0530 (India Standard Time)

| Reply | Reply to All | Forward | Delete | Previous | Next | Compose New | Inbox | Logout |

Dear Raviji, Sudhaji, Sanita and Shubha

Hari Om. Pranams.

I had a wonderful stay at Kannur. It was not just comfortable but also enlightening being with Guruji and inspiring being with you all.

Thank you very much for every thing. Please convey my regards to Pramodji and his family and thanks to Veena amma for making lovely food for Guruji.

Please convey to Sudhaji that I will always remember her yummy food served with lots of love. You are very blessed to have a wonderful wife and very loving children.

You all are invited to Coimbatore. All of us need to spiritually rejuvenate ourselves. 26th of Dec is Deeksha ceremony for the Tamil-English Vedanta course. Please come if it is convenient and also get Sunita. She too will get to meet Guruji.

May Pujya Gurudeva's grace be on all of us so that we continue to work in a Yajna spirit and fulfil the goal of this precious human life.

My special love to Sanita and Shubha.

Wish you all a very Happy New year.

Love

sumati chaitanya

IncrediMail - **Email has finally evolved** - Click Here

SWAMI TEJOMAYANANDA

Kannur

Dec. 17, 2002.

ॐ

Dear Shri. Ravindranath & Sudha,

Hari OM !

Earlier we had met on a formal basis but now after staying with you I have become your family member! I had & such a lovely and pleasant stay with you! Dear Shubha and Sunita added greater glow and joy to my delightful experience. I wish Sunita were also here. Please convey my love and best-wishes to her. Thanks a lot for your love & care.

Herewith is enclosed my next-year's itinerary. Please come to Sidhbari. Greetings to Pramod and Pravish & their families.

Happy New Year !

love & OM,

Tejomayananda

3ᵒ

22-Aug-2001

Dear Sri Ravindranath

Hari Om.

I came back today from Chennai, after three fruitful days there. In addition to the seminar (9:30 am – 4:30 pm) for youth on "Total Success", I spoke at the Institute of Finance Management and Research (IFMR). Sweet memories of my two days at Kannur linger in my mind.

My loving regards and best wishes to Subha, Savitha and to both of you. Hope to meet your eldest child too, some time in the near future.

Please tell your Rotary friends that I enjoyed meeting them.

Hope we shall meet again soon, probably here at the Adi Shankara Nilayam.

Once more, with loving best wishes,

Chidananda.

May Lord bless you all,

Swamini Niranjanananda

Chinmaya Mission
17 Harrington Road
Chetput
Chennai - 600 031
Tel: 8265641

26-11-2001.

To
Sri: Ravindran

Blessed Self,
    Hari om! Salutations.
    This is to express my gratitude for the warm welcome you had extended to me at your lovely home, while I was at Kannur. Please convey my love and thanks to your gracious wife and sweet children. May Gurudev's blessings be on you all!

With Prema om
Sri Niranjanananda.

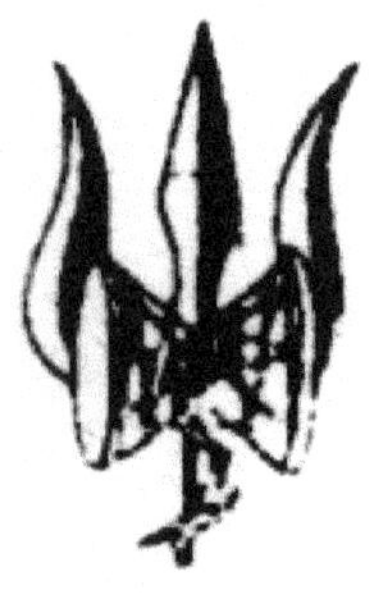

Swamini Vimalananda

Chinmaya Gardens, Nallurvayal (P.O.)
Siruvani Road, Coimbatore - 641 114. India.
Phone : 91 - 422 - 815637 / 815446. Fax : 91 - 422 - 815725.

25.01.2001

To,
Sanita,
"Red Sun"
Beach road – Palliyamoola,
Kannur – 8.

Dear Sanita,

I was so happy to receive your letter and received the lovely card. I'm hoping that you you'll come to Coimbatore in your vacation. Next time I come to Cannanore I will stay in your place if everyone permits. Take care of yourself and family.

With Prem and Om

(Swamini Vimalananda)

Swamini Vimlananda

Chinmaya Gardens, Nallur Vayal (P.O.)
Siruvani Road, Coimbatore - 641 114. India.
Phone : 91 - 422 - 815637 / 815446. Fax : 91 - 422 -815725.

Coimbatore- 641 114
Date : 24.12.00

To,

Shri C.D.Ravindranath
Red Sun, Beach Road
Pallinamulla, Kannur – 670 008.

Dear Shri Ravindranath,

Hari Om !   Namaskaar !!

Thank you for being my *sarathi* throughout the Yagna at Kannur. I was so happy to come to your place and receive *bhiksha* of your dear children. It was a great joy to me that they could attend and enjoy my Yagna in the mornings and evenings. I remember them very much. Please do ask them to write to me. Let the whole family come to Coimbatore sometime.

With Prem and Om to one and all,

VIMALANANDA

Chinmaya Mission
Vidyanagar - 671 123
Kasaragod (Kerala)
Phone: 0499-422429
Fax : 0499-430637
E-mail : vivikta@md4.vsnl.net.in

Sri Raveendranath
Kassm

Date: 24.3.2000

Dear Raveendranathji,

Hari Om!

Trust this finds you, Sudhaji, and the children in the best of spirits. Hope children's exams are going on well. After the exam, the Geeta discussion session has to begin. Now, Apoorvanandadwamini is back in Kassm. Please take the initiative and start it off. Neelu, I am sure, will actively participate. She has promised to give it a try. She is very clean-hearted, though a bit reserved. But she is very intelligent, of which you can be proud. Let her write I shall write to her separately. Let her write the exam well.

Love to all

In the service of the Lord

P.S. The Rakshina amount has been donated to the house construction of a poor, orphaned lady here — one of our Ayahs. Thank you!

Per. No : 430637
Fax : "

Chinmaya Mission
Vidyanagar - 671123
Kasaragod (Kerala)
Phone: (0499)422429

Date: 20 · 1 · 2000

To
Sri Ravindranath
Kanam

Dear Ravindranath Ji,

Hari Om! Salutations!

It was so wonderful to be with you all for some time on Sunday last. I enjoyed every minute of it. And the Bhiksha ... was so sumptuous & tasty. How is Samita now? Hope she has recovered fully.

The Advisory Council meeting was more peaceful, cordial and friendly than last time. We have finalised the Guideline draft, which has been hanging fire for long.

You have a house and a home — and one is as lovely as the other. It is all indeed the Lord's blessings. The 'Lord's Signature' is seen all over in your home!! And may It continue to reign for ever and ever.

With all love & regards to you, wife & children,

In His Service

21-10-99.

Sri. C. V. Ravindranath.
Kannur

Blessed One, Om! Hari Om! Pranam!

I enjoyed every moment of my stay at your Sacred residence with a Divine view of the ocean — roaring & whispering to remind us of 'HIS' Nature to be followed in our Contemplation and Vision embracing with all love, all the waves (Jivas) in 'HIS' Vast expanse to see in depth, the "One" (Silence) in many & many in "ONe". It is thrilling to watch the Ocean and see the Silence within. I was at HOME!

You, your Mrs. (Sudha) especially, and all 3 children (like Ganga-yamuna Saraswati) together looked after this Swami very well with pure love & dedication Divine. I was happy to see that all of them were interested in satsang & sadhana with & for, the Grace of the Lord, besides their studies and hard work. Yajna was a grand success due to whole hearted efforts put forth jointly by C.M./C.V./College, team of dedicated workers for the Cause Divine, under the dynamic & devoted leadership of Shri K.K. Rajan. All of you deserve to be congratulated, in the Grace & blessings of Sri Gurudev!

P. Convey my loveful Harioms to your wife (Mrs. Sudha) & daughters Sumita, Sumita, & Shubha & your brother his own family, in Chinmaya affectionately, with love-Om

swami tejomayananda

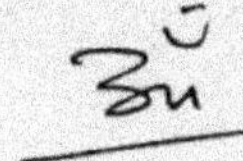

॥ चिदानन्दरूपः शिवोऽहं शिवोऽहम् ॥

Shri C. V. Ravindranath
Red Sun
Palliyamulla Beach
P.O. Alavil
Cannanore 670 008

5th Oct, 1999

Dear Shri Ravindranath,

Hari Om!

Thank you for your letter of 18th Sept. I appreciate your concern for our Vidyalaya in Kannur. It is true that some people try to disturb the atmosphere. But laying down many rules and regulations does not help the situation very much. I feel that the more the rules, the more the problems. If someone is bent on breaking rules, who can stop him! Anyhow, things are now settling down and there is no major problem there.

Thank you for your whole-hearted support towards the management committee.

With love and regards,

Tejomayananda

chinmaya mission 89, lodhi estate, new-delhi 110003, tel: 4697848.

CHINMAYA MISSION ®

Swami Tejomayananda

ॐ

Camp: Trinidad
7.7.99.

Dear Shri. Ravindranath,

Hari OM!

Thank you for your kind letter dated 12th of June. My hectic travel schedule delayed its acknowledgement.

Noted the contents of your letter to Mr. Bill Clinton. I appreciate your concern for the World Peace and your initiative in that direction. May God bless all with simple Commonsense to live in peace together !

Thanks for your appreciation of my discourses.

with Best wishes.

Tejomayananda

SWAMI TEJOMAYANANDA

ॐ

Camp: Dar-Es-Salaam,
Tanzania.
2.9.99.

Dear Shri. Ravindranath,

Hari OM!

Thanks for your two letters dated 12th and 15th of August.

I was glad to know about the appreciation of your article. It was nice of you to send copies of Tapovan Prasad to dignitories. I liked the article "Jai Jawan". As long as powerful countries sponsor terrorism, this evil cannot be eradicated completely. May God bless all with noble feelings and thoughts.

With Prem & OM,

Tejomayananda

दूरभाष : (००–६१) (०११) ६९७८८६२, ६९०३४५५
फैक्स : ६१-११-६९६५५२७
तार : हिन्दूधर्म

Phones : (00-91)(011) 6103495, 6178992
Fax : 6195527, 3792896
E-Mail : samvad @del2.vsnl.net.in
Gram : 'HINDUDHARMA'

विश्व हिन्दू परिषद
VISHVA HINDU PARISHAD

Registered Under Societies Registration Act 1860 No. S 3106 of 1966-67 with Registrar of Societies, Delhi

संकट मोचन आश्रम, (हनुमान मंदिर) सेक्टर-६, रामकृष्णपुरम्, नई दिल्ली – ११००२२ (भारत)
Sankat Mochan Ashram, Ramakrishna Puram-VI, New Delhi - 110022 (Bharat)

पत्र संख्या Ref. No.   दिनांक Dated :

VHP/ २ /99.   Date: 26-2-99.

अध्यक्ष
विष्णु हरि डालमिया
President
'''' Dalmia

कार्याध्यक्ष
अशोक सिंहल
Working President
Ashok Singhal

उपाध्यक्ष (केन्द्रीय)
डा. सुजीत धर
Vice President (Central)
Dr. Sujit Dhar

महामंत्री
आचार्य गिरिराज किशोर,
Secretary General
Acharya Giriraj Kishore

संयुक्त महामंत्री
सदानन्द काकडे
ओंकार भावे
कृष्ण नाईक
Joint General Secretary
Sadananda Kakade
Omkar Bhaway
Balkrishna Naik

Aadarniya Shri Pramod Ji Mahajan,
Minister for Information and Broadcasting,
Central Government of India, New Delhi.

Sub: <u>Maha Shivratri Mahotsava</u>

On the above subject a letter dt. 15-2-99 from Shri C.V. Ravindranath Ji is received in V.H.P. office inviting our attention to the dismal manner in which the celebration of Maha Shivratri was telecast.

The original letter is enclosed for your perusal.

It is hoped you will take cognisance of such festivity which inspires the society as a whole to adapt itself to the infinite moral values in life conducive to the welfare of human race in this universe without any distinction, no matter the people follow their faith in the manner they deem it the sound basis of eternal Truth practising of which they may get salvation of bondage in worldly life.

It is urged to initiate comprehensive rationalised programmes of having cohesive moral values in nature, rising above any prejudice in this regard. Justification done to such festivity tending integrated moral impetus on the people is of great value so that the people of motley culture may live in social harmony without any fear.

Hoping your functioning cooperation.

Yours Sincerely,

(Ashok Singhal)
Working President, V.H.P.

VHP/2/99
Copy to:
Shri C.V. Ravindranath ji,
Red Sun,
Palliyamulla Beach,
P.O. Alavil,
Kannur-670008

MAHARISHI INSTITUTE OF MANAGEMENT

P.T.C. Colony Pallavan Nagar Thiruverkadu Chennai 600 077 INDIA
E.MAIL smruti@giasmd01.vsnl.net.in   WEBSITE ADDRESS http://www.mum.edu/
TELEPHONE 091- 044 - 6273921, 6273190, 6272221   TELEFAX 091 - 044 - 6413711

C.V. Ravindranath
Managing Partner
Kunhikannan Jewellery Gold House
Cannanore 670 001

My dear Ravindranath,

I apologize for the horrendous delay in getting back to you, but I fear such is the nature of my activities that only today after a delay of six months am I finally getting some photos off to my son in California.

I'm enclosing information on Modern Science & Vedic Science, though the prices appear most high for India. However, there are several books by Maharishi now available through TM centers in India. One, in particular, I recommend highly — "Celebrating Perfection in Education". It is in a 8½" × 11" format and is very concise yet overflowing in knowledge.

Since I don't know where Cannanore is located in Kerala — no, I just looked at a map & see that my proposed suggestion of Cochin for the nearest center is flawed. Instead I believe that we have a facility, possibly a Maharishi Vidya Mandir in Shoranur & also a center in Mangalore or nearby in Udipi.

Sincerely,
Jim Brown

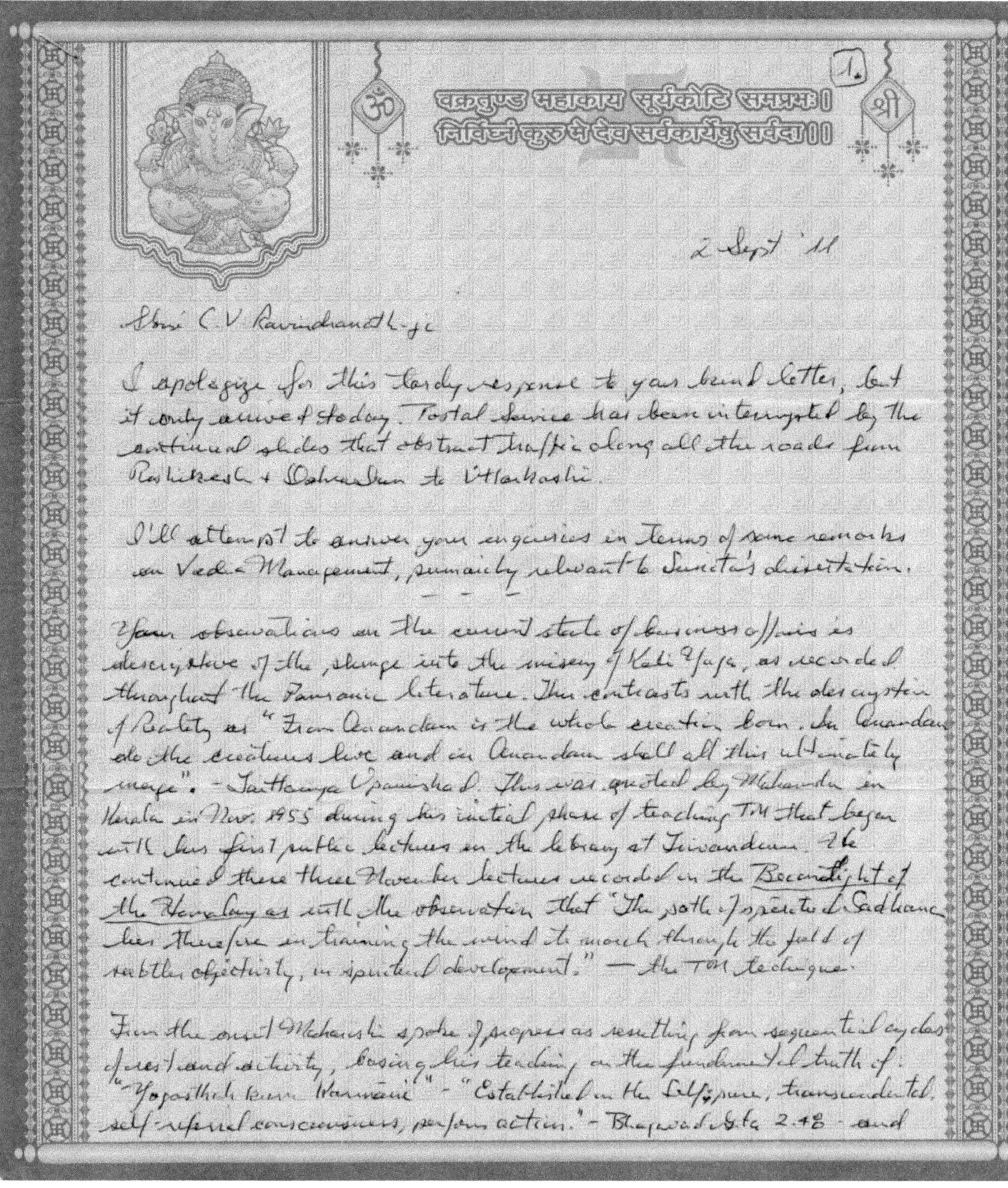

2 Sept '11

Shri C.V. Ravindranath-ji

I apologize for this tardy response to your kind letter, but it only arrived today. Postal Service has been interrupted by the continual slides that obstruct traffic along all the roads from Rishikesh & Dehradun to Uttarkashi.

I'll attempt to answer your enquiries in terms of some remarks on Vedic Management, primarily relevant to Sunita's dissertation.

— — —

Your observations on the current state of business affairs is descriptive of the plunge into the misery of Kali Yuga, as recorded throughout the Puranic literature. This contrasts with the description of Reality as "From Anandam is the whole creation born. In Anandam do the creatures live and in Anandam shall all this ultimately merge". – Taittireya Upanishad. This was quoted by Maharishi in Kerala in Nov. 1955 during his initial phase of teaching TM that began with his first public lectures in the library at Trivandrum. He continued these three November lectures recorded in the Beacon Light of the Himalayas as well the observation that "The path of spiritual Sadhana lies therefore in training the mind to march through the field of subtler objectivity, in spiritual development." — the TM technique.

From the onset Maharishi spoke of progress as resulting from sequential cycles of rest and activity, basing his teaching on the fundamental truth of: "Yogasthah kuru karmani" – "Established in the Self, pure, transcendental, self-referral consciousness, perform action." – Bhagavad Gita 2.48 - and

"Prakritim svam avashtabhya visrijāmi punah punah" - "Self-referral tendency of pure consciousness (curving back onto My Nature) gives rise to the creative process." - Bhagavad Gita 9.8 These two principles are repeated in his titles for the years 1990 & 1991: "Alliance with Nature's Government" and "Support of Nature's Government" and culminate in the simultaneity of "Yatinām Brahma bhavati sāra kila" - "For those established in self-referral consciousness, the infinite organizing power of the Creator becomes the charioteer of all action." - Rk Veda 1.158.6 - Purusha and Prakriti merged as Purushottam, the Administrator, administering through silence, as exemplified for our age by Maharaj Adhiraj Raja Raam, the first sovereign ruler of the Global Country of World Peace. Thus perhaps be fittingly I first refer Sumita to Maharajaji's book Human Physiology, which MIU-Chennai should have.

These principles inform one how to be a Vedic manager and contain in seed form the understanding both how to become a Vedic manager and what is Vedic management.

When Lord Krishna departed from earth, marking the onset of Kali Yuga, the eternal, non-changing, transcendental Reality, experienced as Transcendental Consciousness (TC) became overshadowed, 'hidden', 'covered' by the chandas value of life, which became experienced solely as a cycle of waking, dreaming, and sleeping states of consciousness. Adharma eliminated as the evolutionary force of Dharma was reduced to 25%, resulting in the creations of problems and suffering that plague Kali Yuga.

To rescue mankind from this misery, 'to avert the danger that has not yet come' Yoga Sutra II.16, His Divinity Brahmananda Saraswati, Shankaracharya of Jyotir Math, Maharishi's Master blessed the world with the supreme gift of the technique of transcending and "opened the door to Perfection" that the realization of Atma became available to everyone. Maharishi for fifty years ceaselessly carried this message of perfection in life and the means for growing in this awareness of Totality throughout the world. He taught the Transcendental Meditation and TM-Sidhis programs, including Yogic Flying, reenlivened the forty branches of the Veda and Vedic literature, and established a Global Country of World

Peace to usher in and maintain a Vedic civilization based upon the purity of the knowledge he had received from Guru Dev.

Thus, how to become a Vedic manager is to transcend, to transcend and continue to infuse greater silence into the dynamism of one's activities, until the full infinite value of silence is maintained and pure knowledge with its infinite organizing power, Veda, is fully expressed in every action: Tat Brahma becomes the character. Veda is the structuring dynamic of Atma. Awareness established in Atma, life in Silence, is expressed in the purity of Veda; no mistakes or problems are created, only life-supporting influences emerge. The process by which one becomes a Vedic manager, as Maharishi has emphasized, is to transcend and then come out into activity with increasing ability "to do less and accomplish more", until one is able to do, practically nothing and accomplish everything.

What is Vedic management has been unfolded by Maharishi in his books and lectures. The beauty of the life of such a saint is not merely in the knowledge he brings out, but also, as importantly, in his ability to know when and how it should be expressed, so that it is properly understood. 'Knowledge is structured in Consciousness', the motto of MUM, and the saying that 'a little knowledge is a dangerous thing' are indications that knowledge beyond the experience of the student can give rise to misinterpretations that lead to practices damaging to his evolution, so as mood-making.

Maharishi from the onset emphasized the experiential value of knowledge along with its intellectual understanding. Thus, only after continual practice of his TM-Sidhi Program, (perhaps when collective consciousness as well as individual consciousness was sufficiently...

purified) did he introduce Maharishi's Vedic Science, did he speak fully
in terms of Advaita Vedant. This knowledge he brought forth layer by layer
in expanded versions. The knowledge he expanded in his Apaurusheya Bhashya
of Rik Veda, the self-commentary of nitya and apaurusheya Veda, eternal and
uncreated Veda. This provided the knowledge of the "Constitution of the Universe",
the foundational level of all the laws of Nature that govern the universe, the
source of Dharma, the Veda. This is Vedic Management, management by that
supreme intelligence that governs the entire galactic universe, that "Automation
in Administration" that silently ensures that every particle of creation evolves in
an orderly, progressive fashion.

Thus to properly comprehend Vedic Management one should not take recourse to some,
perhaps uninformed, interpretation of Maharishi's teaching. but should
read and listen to his words directly. Thus I recommend the following:

1. <u>Celebrating Perfection in Education</u>: Dawn of Total Knowledge,
   and then particularly the extensive footnotes in:
2. <u>Maharishi's Absolute Theory of Government</u>: Automation in Administration,
3. <u>Maharishi's Absolute Theory of Defense</u>: Sovereignty in Invincibility, and
4. <u>Maharishi Vedic University</u>: Introduction

Again all should be in the library at MUM – Chennai (and all too
infrequently consulted).

Though this knowledge is beautifully presented, for instance, in the Ramayana
and Shrimad Bhagavata Mahapurana, and also with respect to Kashmiri
Shaivism in the writings of Swami Lakshman Joo, nowhere have I found
such complete, self-consistent descriptions as those found in Maharishi's books
and lectures, and, moreover, in terms not only fully expressive of Advaita Vedanta,
but accessible as well to the intellects that we of Kali Yuga possess. At the
same time he writes both in today's and in awareness of language.

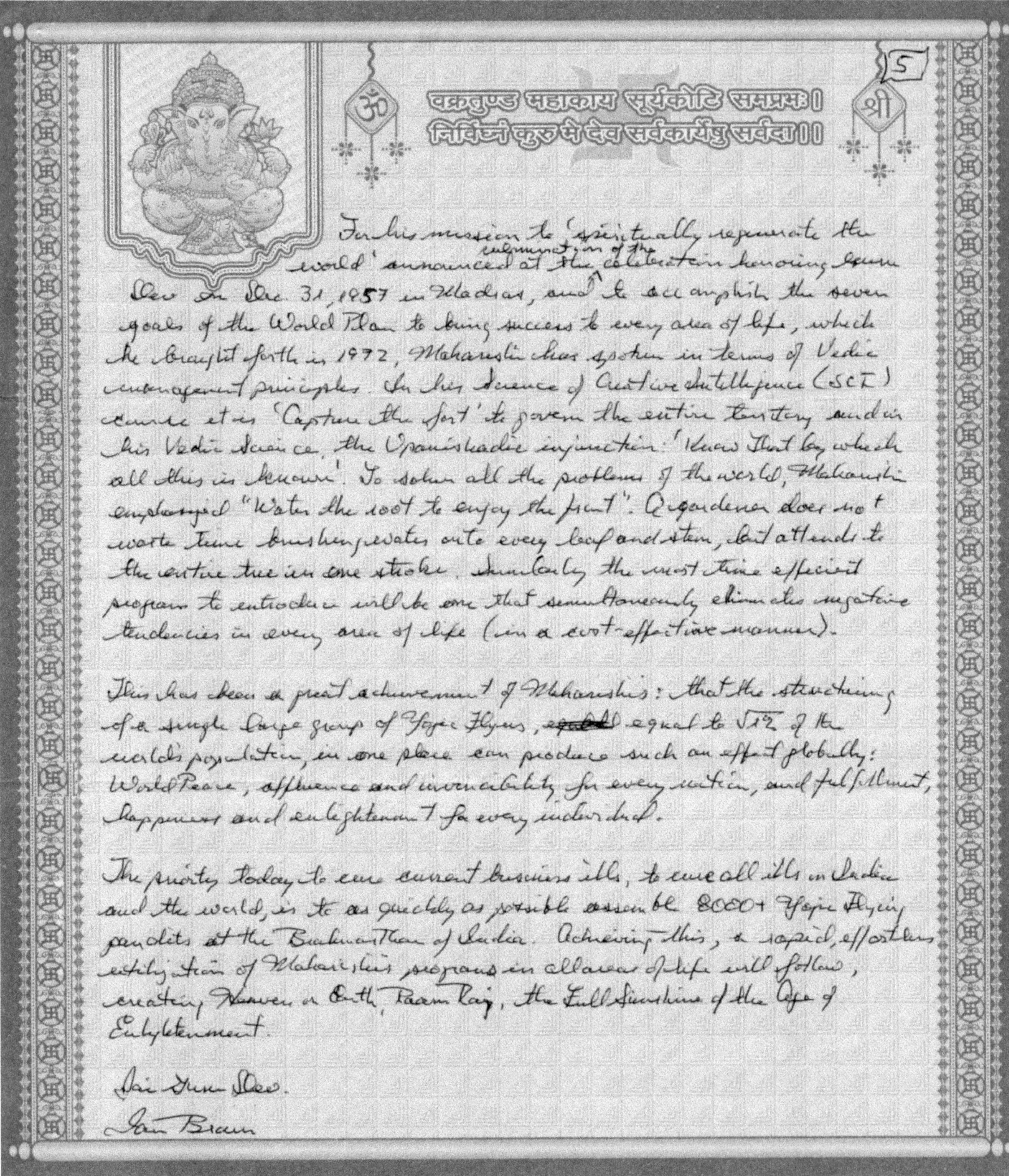

वक्रतुण्ड महाकाय सूर्यकोटि समप्रभः ।
निर्विघ्नं कुरु मे देव सर्वकार्येषु सर्वदा ॥

For his mission to 'spiritually regenerate the world' announced at the celebration honoring Guru Dev On Dec 31, 1957 in Madras, and to accomplish the seven goals of the World Plan to bring success to every area of life, which he brought forth in 1972, Maharishi has spoken in terms of Vedic management principles. In his Science of Creative Intelligence (SCI) course it is 'Capture the fort' to govern the entire territory, and in his Vedic Science, the Upanishadic injunction: 'Know That by which all this is known'. To solve all the problems of the world, Maharishi emphasized "Water the root to enjoy the fruit". A gardener does not waste time brushing water onto every leaf and stem, but attends to the entire tree in one stroke. Similarly the most time efficient program to introduce will be one that simultaneously eliminates negative tendencies in every area of life (in a cost-effective manner).

This has been a great achievement of Maharishi's: that the structuring of a single large group of Yogic Flyers, equal to $\sqrt{1\%}$ of the world's population, in one place can produce such an effect globally: World Peace, affluence and invincibility for every nation, and fulfillment, happiness and enlightenment for every individual.

The priority today to cure current business ills, to cure all ills in India and the world, is to as quickly as possible assemble 8000+ Yogic Flying pandits at the Brahmasthan of India. Achieving this, a rapid, effortless enlivening of Maharishi's programs in all areas of life will follow, creating Heaven on Earth, Raam Raj, the Full Sunshine of the Age of Enlightenment.

Jai Guru Dev.

Ian Braun

Swami Tejomayananda

Chinmaya Dhyana Nilayam
Consecrated on **15.02.1999**

Date : 15.2.99.

Dear Shri. Ravindranathji,

Hari OM!

Thanks for your letter dated 29th of January received along with your beautiful article on "Secret of Success in Business". I enjoyed reading it and was impressed by your assimilation of Pujya Gurudev's Teachings in general and his thoughts on the topic of Management. Hearty Congratulations! May you attain greater and greater success with God and Gurudev on your side!

Love,
Tejomayananda

Camp :
C/o Smt. Malleswari
6-3-1195/A, Uma Nagar.
Begumpet. Hyderabad - 500 016.
Phone : 040-3312915

Most Honourable +
respected Poojya Gurudev
Swami Chinmayanandji

Season's Greetings

and Best Wishes

for a Happy

and Prosperous

New Year

We pray for your
Health Gurudev

Chinmayam
Sredhalari
9 Jan 1992

O. V. RAVINDRANATH
CHINMAYA MISSION
KANNUR

KUNHIKANNAN JEWELLERY
KANNUR - 670001.
Phone : 67175 / 66467 / 65032 (Shop)
66767 / 68503 (Res)

CHINMAYA MISSION PERTH

35 Gladstone Road
Kalamunda
Western Australia 6076
30 April 1990.
Phone: (09) 293 2732

Sri. P.V. Ravindranatha,
Flat 11, Bldgs 322,
Road 1805, Manama.
3/8 Baharain
≡ Arabian Gulf ≡

Harorrs! Salutations!!
If I were you I will explain and pursuade the wife to see reason. After 4-5 years of work you can go back to India. Now let the child be in C. V. dzalaya, and wife can visit-you every other year. This is how people struggle in the early years!

Love,

P.S. You may also get some free flight in Plane to India now & then.

Ravindranath C.V <sudhacvr@gmail.com>

Maha Meru Mandhir at Sarveshwara Dhama

dk sreenath <dk_sreenath_1508@yahoo.com>   Tue, Dec 19, 2023 at 9:14 AM
To: "sudhacvr@gmail.com" <sudhacvr@gmail.com>
Cc: Rishi Sanjeevini <swmission2007@gmail.com>

Sir,
Namaskaram !
I am Srinath, one of the Devotees of Mathaji Dr.Sripriya. I have been asked to co-ordinate for The Maha Meru Mandhir in Sarveshwara Dhama. Regarding the same, I would like to share a few things with your Good Self :
After receiving your mail, Amma interacted with Adi Parashakthi Amma and Sri Ganesha and the revelations were as follows :
- Maha Meru to be made in Krishna Shila.
- Only Dr.Sri.Ravindranath to be consulted for this Purpose.
- Estimate to be taken for Maha Meru as per the design of Dr.Sri.Ravindranath.

Based on this interaction, I would add a few more things.
Sri.Jagannath was an architect only for the Temple. We cannot consult him for Maha Meru. Moreover, as per the Divine Dictum Dr.Sri.Ravindranath will be the only point of contact for this purpose.
So we request you to kindly talk to the Shilpi and get an estimate for Maha Meru made of Krishna Shila.

With Regards, I remain

Always under the Divine Lotus Feet of Amma !

D.K.Srinath

Gmail - Place for installation of Maha Meru   https://mail.google.com/mail/u/0/?ik=ddcebe07c6&view=pt&search=al...

 Gmail

Ravindranath C.V <sudhacvr@gmail.com>

Place for installation of Maha Meru

Rishi Sanjeevini <swmission2007@gmail.com>   Fri, Dec 15, 2023 at 10:58 PM
To: ravindranath <sudhacvr@gmail.com>

Dearest beta namaste

Today is the 77 th day of my Soundaryalahari Yagam . Two days back all the trustees of Shakthiveda Wellness Mission decided to install Mahameru at Sarveshwaradhama . It was WILL of Supreme Goddess supported by all the divine energies. I have attached the drawing of the existing building in which Amma's Maha Meru will be installed. I humbly request your support in making according to golden ratio. Please guide us as we don't know much about technical aspect of it . It shoukd be grand and powerful . Please suggest according to the measurement .

We all wish to visit you after my 100 days Soundaryalahari Tagam which is scheduled to culminate on 7 th Jan 2024 for the same reason. Thank you

with gratitude
Amma

 **SADGURU MANDIRA.pdf**
369K

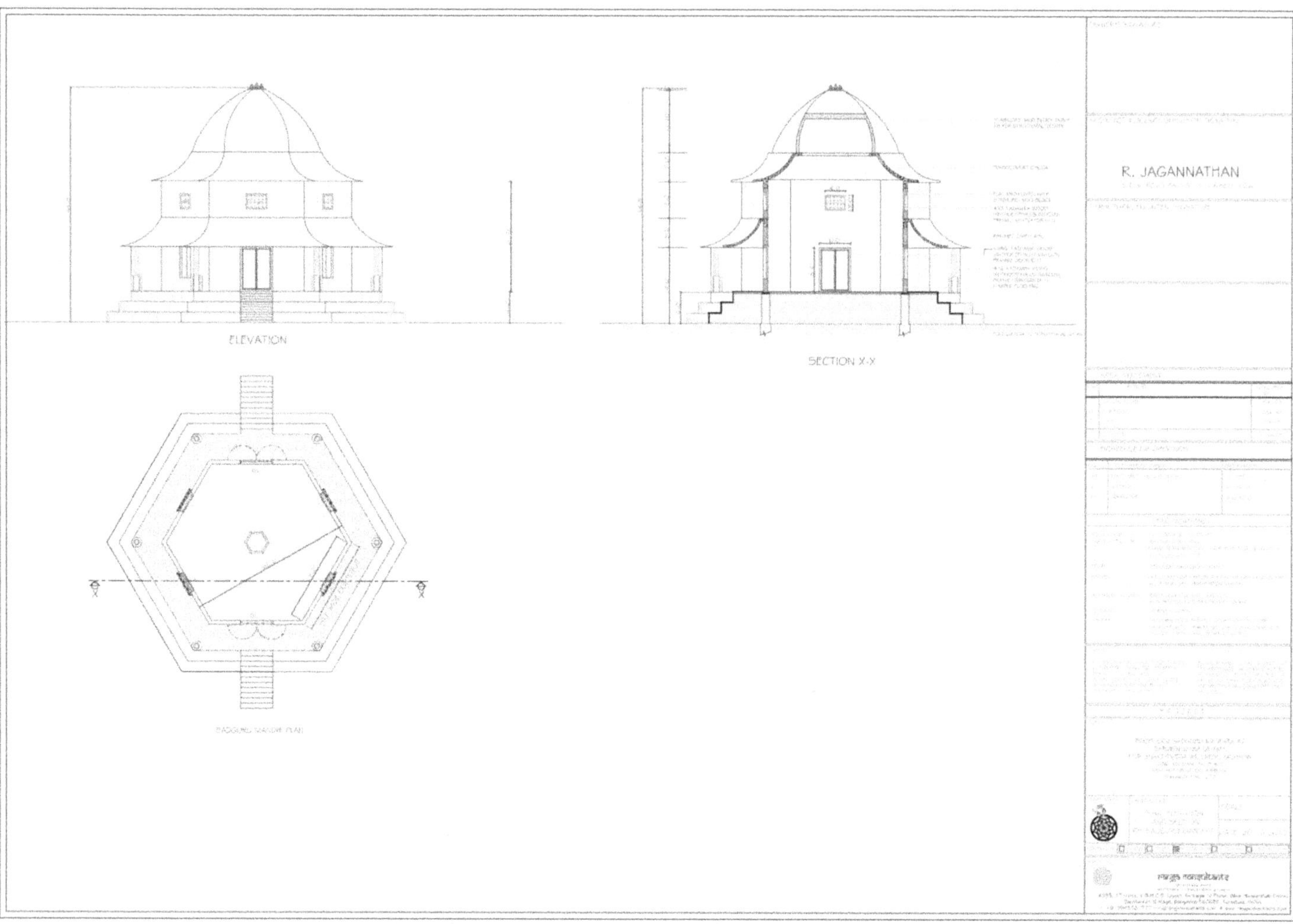

CHAPTER III

HEALTH IS WEALTH

For the good Health of Body, Mind & Soul, we require advices from great people in the field of Medical Care and Support.

We have 5 letters of hope from 9.6.2020 to 16.10.2023, which had helped me to strive after Ramsay Hunt Syndrome stroke in 2016.

Ravindranath C.V <sudhacvr@gmail.com>

Medical Care for Cerebrospinal Fluid Leakage (CSF) causing Auto Rhinorrhea

Web Information Manager <webmanager-ayush@gov.in>   Mon, Oct 16, 2023 at 4:43 PM
To: sudhacvr@gmail.com

Sir/Madam,

   The CSF is a clear, colorless fluid that occupies the ventricular system, the cerebral and spinal subarachnoid spaces, and the perivascular spaces in the CNS. The fluid is a mixture of water, proteins at low concentrations, ions, neurotransmitters, and glucose that is renewed three to four times per day (Damkier et al., 2013; Hladky and Barrand, 2014; Spector et al., 2015). Several theories have been proposed to explain how CSF is produced. The classic theory states that the choroid plexus are the primary sources of CSF production. The CSF flow dynamics within the ventricular system and the subarachnoid spaces is thought to consist of two main types of movements: convective flow and pulsatile flow

सादर / Regards,

वेब सूचना प्रबंधक / Web Information Manager,
आयुष मंत्रालय, भारत सरकार / Ministry of Ayush, Govt. of India
आयुष भवन / AYUSH Bhawan
बी-ब्लॉक, जी.पी.ओ. काम्प्लेक्स / B- Block, G.P.O. Complex
आई.एन.ए., नई दिल्ली - 110023 / I.N.A., New Delhi - 110023

From: sudhacvr@gmail.com
To: "Web Information Manager" <webmanager-ayush@gov.in>, dsenthil@ias.nic.in
Sent: Thursday, September 28, 2023 5:16:10 PM
Subject: Medical Care for Cerebrospinal Fluid Leakage (CSF) causing Auto Rhinorrhea
[Quoted text hidden]

Ravindranath C.V <sudhacvr@gmail.com>

Tantric Management – Part 1- SECRET OF SUCCESS !

Jill <drjill@drjilltaylor.com>   Wed, Feb 8, 2023 at 10:10 PM
To: "Ravindranath C.V" <sudhacvr@gmail.com>

Hello respected one:

I agree that "I"ness when it is not balanced brings illness - but it also brings functionality.

I believe the universe has created a brilliant design that it both the I and the WE on purpose. The ultimate goal should be a balance between the two, not just one over the other. Neither alone is healthy. To not value any of our designed parts is an oversight into the big picture of how we function as a human being and whole brain. I will agree that it is important that we function from the VALUEs of the WE, but to not recognize the gifts and value of the 'I' is to overlook that it:

1. Defines the boundaries of our physical structure so we can organize ourselves as functional beings
2. Gives us language so we can communicate verbally
3. Gives us linearity of thought so we can learn from our mistakes
4. Gives us order so that we are functional in relation to the external world
5. Gives us deep emotion so we can attach and care about one another

Without individuality we exist and live in chaos - based on the skill-sets of our brain. I think we can agree that the ultimate goal should be living life from the value of the 'WE' but exist in balance using our 'I' to support the 'WE'?

Warmly, Jill

Dr. Jill Bolte Taylor
drjill@drjilltaylor.com
Author My Stroke of Insight and Whole Brain Living
Time 100 Most Influential

"Please take responsibility for the energy you bring into this space."

On Feb 6, 2023, at 3:14 AM, Ravindranath C.V <sudhacvr@gmail.com> wrote:

 Gmail   **Ravindranath C.V <sudhacvr@gmail.com>**

Re: Dr. Jill Contact Form Submission

Jill <drjill@drjilltaylor.com>   Thu, Jan 12, 2023 at 9:08 PM
To: sudhacvr@gmail.com

Dear Sir, creating a brain bank is a very expensive, space and time consuming project.

I know other countries have brain banks but the US system is separate from those due to controlling as many variables as possible. The brain banks in the US specialize in specific types of disorders - Alzheimer, schizophrenia, Huntington's, children's tissue, etc.

You should also note that collecting brains that have active virus remain contagious to those who handle that tissue. This would require special treatment. My guess is that your local scientists who want to study Covid are already collecting that tissue from the local coroners or pathologists?

I am no longer at the Harvard Brain Bank - as all brain banking has been taken over and centralized by the US government, a few years ago. If you would like to pursue the idea of creating a brain bank in India that is not affiliated with the Harvard Brain Bank then please call them directly at 1-800-brainbank and I'm sure they will be able to put you in touch with the centralized US banking authorities.

Thank you, Jill

Dr. Jill Bolte Taylor
drjill@drjilltaylor.com
Author My Stroke of Insight and Whole Brain Living
Time 100 Most Influential

"Please take responsibility for the energy you bring into this space."

On Jan 12, 2023, at 6:45 AM, Dr. Jill Bolte Taylor <drjill@drjilltaylor.com> wrote:

From: Dr C V Ravindranath
Email: <sudhacvr@gmail.com>
Subject: drjill@drjilltaylor.com

Message:
Respected Madam,

Hare Krishna!

cv Ravindranth

From:	Jill [drjill@drjilltaylor.com]
Sent:	Monday, January 16, 2023 9:27 PM
To:	Ravindranath C.V
Subject:	Re: Brain MRI report

Hello friend, what do I call you, what is your first name?

I am not a medical doctor so I cannot give you medical advice, but I did take a look at your pathology report and it is looking pretty good. You had a stroke - but they don't report where that happened or problems directly associated with it. Ramsay Hunt Syndrome is of course of viral origin and anything related to your head/face would most likely be related to that.

First, I can share with you that alpha lipoic acid interfered with my mother's sleeping - so you might explore the medicines you are taking and observe how they influence the sleep cycle. Once you start sleeping better then the body will begin to heal again naturally. Sleep is so important for everything as it is the time that the body cleanses out the waste from the cellular activity - and all parts of our body need that daily flush.

If I were in your position I would drink hot water with a thumb's worth of ginger and turmeric - as strong as you can stand it - at least once a day but really ongoing throughout the day. These are major anti-inflammatory foods and excellent for your digestion and abdomen. There are lists of anti-inflammatory foods on the internet that might help you. That is where I would begin.

The Top 20 Anti-Inflammatory Foods
blog.silvercuisine.com

Again, I am not a medical doctor and cannot give you medical advice, but I do wish you all the very best along your journey.

Warmly, Jill

Dr. Jill Bolte Taylor
drjill@drjilltaylor.com
Author My Stroke of Insight and Whole Brain Living
Time 100 Most Influential

"Please take responsibility for the energy you bring into this space."

On Jan 16, 2023, at 3:19 AM, Ravindranath C.V <sudhacvr@gmail.com> wrote:

The Top 20 Anti-Inflammation Foods

1. Avocados

Avocados are unique in the fact they are rich in healthy fat, unlike most fruits that naturally supply carbohydrate. They also source a number of antioxidants, including lutein and zeaxanthin that can protect the eyes from cataracts and macular degeneration, common conditions in the elderly. Avocadoes have been shown to reduce inflammation in young skin cells, along with managing blood pressure and promoting digestive health relative to its high fiber and potassium concentrations.

2. Blueberries

They may be small, but blueberries are nothing short of mighty. Blueberries are chock-full of fiber, vitamins, and minerals, along with supplying antioxidants such as anthocyanins, gallic acid, and resveratrol. The compounds can help combat against inflammation, boost immunity, reduce heart disease risk, and improve skin health. Strawberries, blackberries, raspberries, and other colorful berries are also suppliers of powerful antioxidants.

3. Beets

The deep and rich color of beets is not only eye-appealing, but signifies its potent antioxidant content. Beets contain betalain, a pigment supplying their signature color and an excellent anti-inflammatory. Primarily related to its nitrate content, research additionally shows drinking beet juice may fight the progression of dementia. Nitrites have shown to widen blood vessels, thus increasing oxygen-rich blood flow to the brain.

4. Bone Broth

Bone broth is created by simmering together water, animal bones, vegetables, and various seasonings, with the long and slow process releasing valuable minerals from the bones and collagen from the joints. Largely in the form of minerals, antioxidants in bone broth may demonstrate the power to fight against aging by protecting the body from damaging free radicals, harmful compounds mostly originating from environmental toxins or stemming from a poor diet.

5. Broccoli

As if there was just another reason to eat your broccoli... The cruciferous veggie supplies potent antioxidants, including sulforaphane. The antioxidant has shown to fight inflammation by reducing levels of cytokines, signaling proteins shown to synergize inflammation. Research has also shown consuming cruciferous vegetables, including cauliflower and Brussels sprouts, is associated with a decreased risk of both heart disease and cancer.

6. Cherries

Cherries are one of the best foods to reduce inflammation, with researchers suggesting both tart and sweet variations display the highest anti-inflammatory content of any food! They are packed with antioxidants, such as anthocyanins and catechins, which can lower inflammation related to arthritis and muscle recovery.

7. Coffee

Reaching for that morning cup of joe not only gifts that energy jolt, but supplies powerful antioxidants. Along with reducing inflammation, coffee is tied to better brain health and may enhance memory, reduce dementia risk, lower the risk of Parkinson's disease, and stave off depression. However, it is important to divvy away from copious amounts of added sugars and creams, as they can be pro-inflammatory and dismiss the benefits of coffee.

8. Dark Chocolate

Simultaneously kick the craving and up the antioxidants! Dark chocolate contains polyphenols are powerful antioxidants, showing to lower the risk of cardiovascular disease, certain cancers, and brain deterioration. But to have your chocolate and eat it too, it is important to keep sugar minimized; use cocoa powder in cooking and look for dark chocolate products with minimal added sugars.

9. Fatty Fish

Including salmon, anchovies, herring, mackerel, tuna, and sardines, fatty fish are rich in omega-3 fatty acids. Fatty fish contain high amounts of the omega-3 fatty acids eicosapentaenoic acid (EPA) and docosahexaenoic acid (DHA), which offers anti-inflammatory effects to the body.

10. Flax and Chia Seeds

Not a fan of fish? Both flax and chia seeds seeds are likewise rich in omega-3 fatty acids, along with being a valuable plant-based protein and fiber source. So in addition to reducing inflammation in the body, these seeds support digestive and heart health.

11. Grapes

Several plant compounds in grapes, including flavonoids and resveratrol, can reduce inflammation and protect against damage, particularly related to cardiovascular disease, diabetes, and Alzheimer's disease.

12. Green Tea

Going green with your tea pours out bountiful health benefits, mostly related to its catechin content, a type of polyphenol. Green tea has demonstrated to reduce inflammation and protect cells from damage that may lead to disease, including diabetes, heart disease, and cancer. Regular consumption may also assist in weight loss efforts by increasing metabolism and reducing fat mass.

13. Leafy Greens

Leafy greens are extremely high in polyphenols and vitamins A, C, and K, all of which are believed to offer anti-inflammatory properties. From spinach to kale, add leafy greens to a number of meals, including salads, soups, casseroles, and soups.

14. Nuts

Almonds, walnuts, and other nut varieties are rich in healthy fat shown to combat against inflammation. In fact, evidence correlate nuts with reduced markers of inflammation, along with a lower risk of cardiovascular disease and diabetes. Nuts are also rich in protein and fiber, two dietary components that facilitate and accelerate weight loss efforts.

15. Oats

Oats are a whole grain that seem to have special health properties, notoriously known for its role in digestive and heart health thanks to its high fiber content. However, oats also contain compounds known as avenanthramides, which have shown to offer anti-inflammatory and antioxidant properties. So rather than pouring out a sugary bowl of cereal in the morning, prepare these overnight oat recipes for significant health benefits.

16. Olive Oil

Along with supplying heart-healthy monounsaturated fat, olive oil is a known source of oleocanthal, a phenolic compound shown to offer anti-inflammatory benefits. In fact, oleocanthal has exhibited the same anti-inflammatory response in the body as NSAID ibuprofen, designating it as a safe and natural anti-inflammatory agent.

17. Oranges

Oranges are notorious for their vitamin C content, which can act as a potent antioxidant. Vitamin C helps to reduce the damage from ultraviolet (UV) light exposure, a major risk factor for skin cancer. The vitamin has also shown to reduce skin wrinkling and improve overall skin appearance, while it's collagen-building properties shape and maintain the structure of bone, tendon, skin, cartilage and all other connective tissue.

18. Red Wine

Being produced from grapes, red wine is notorious for its resveratrol content. Resveratrol becomes more concentrated during the fermentation process, while being more potent in red over white wine. Researchers have correlated resveratrol to numerous health advantages, including good heart health, cancer prevention, and anti-aging. To reap the most benefit of red wine, drink in moderation and verify its consumption will not cause adverse side effects related to medication interactions.

19. Tomatoes

Tomatoes are an excellent source of lycopene, a carotenoid found in pink and red plants. The color-producing pigment has also shown to protect against inflammation, cancer, and skin damage caused by ultraviolet (UV) light that shines from the sun.

20. Turmeric

While not a food per se, turmeric is certainly worth mentioning. Coming from the turmeric plant, turmeric is a spice bright in color and mostly known for its warm, bitter taste in curry dishes. In addition to its culinary use, turmeric has been used to treat an extensive number of inflammatory and infectious diseases and conditions, particularly related to its curcumin content. Curcumin, the chemical providing the vibrant color of turmeric, is suggested to reduce inflammation and combat against infection.

DEAR ALL,

I WOULD LIKE TO EXPRESS MY THANKS AND APPRECIATION FOR THE SERVICE AND CARE,THAT WE HAD RECEIVED AT KRISHNA BEACH RESORT DURING OUR QUARANTINE PERIOD FROM 01/06/2020 TO 08/06/2020

YOUR HOTEL PROVIDED GREAT QUALITY SERVICES AND ROOM WAS VERY COMFORTABLEAND CLEAN.
THE HOTEL TEAM HAD DEFINITELY DEVOTE THEIR BEST EFFORTS IN SHOWING THEIR CONCERNED FOR OUR COMFORT

SPECIAL THANKS AGAIN TO VOLUNTEERS, MANAGEMENT , AND CO-OPERATION FOR GIVING SUCH A GREAT SUPPORT
AND FACILITIES FOR ALL MIGRANT PEOPLES LIKE ME
WE HAD A WONDERFUL QUARANTINE, AND I HAVE RECOMMENDED KRISHNA BEACH RESORT TO ALL OF MY COLLEAGUES, FRIENDS AND FAMILY.

THANK YOU AGAIN FOR SUCH OUTSTANDING SERVICE.

Muhammad Ali

9567 75 75 67
Taliparamba
Room no:103

CHAPTER IV

POSITIVITY IN BUSINESS

We get positive energy to do business through Motivation and Inspiration from great scholars of our times, promoting IQ and EQ in business management.

Here, we have 20 letters from 27.8.1991 to 22.2.2024 to boost our self-confidence.

O.V. RADHAKRISHNAN
SENIOR ADVOCATE

RADHA & RADHA
ADVOCATES

Dear Dr. Ravindranath,

Sorry for the delay in responding to your warm and affectionate letter dated 12-04-2023. Indeed your remarkable and greatest achievement in bringing out the World First Resort built on Tantric Vaasthu Shilpa Shastra inculcating Spiritual Tourism for the rejuvenation of the Body, Mind and Soul through Ayurveda, Yoga and Tantra is praiseworthy.

I have gone through the brochures of Krishna Beach Resort and Krishna Jewels, containing pictures and information on your Resort and Krishna Jewels. You can always rest assured my patronage in all respects.

I express my profound thankfulness for your kind invitation for a stay at Krishna Beach Resort.

Your Vishu gift of the book "Ectasy of Beauty – A prayer to mother Nature" and the article "The effect of Shiva Shakti Mahameru on human energy field" are undeniably great works expressing the spiritual dimension of human experience.

With warmest regards,

Respectfully Yours,

O.V.Radhakrishnan

Ernakulam,
17-04-2023.

OLD RAILWAY STATION ROAD, PROVIDENCE POINT, KOCHI - 682 018.
MOBILE NO. 9446765777, OFF:0484-2390318. RES:0484-2390686

From:	jerry amaldev [devamaljerry@gmail.com]
Sent:	Wednesday, February 15, 2023 10:49 AM
To:	ravindranath
Subject:	How are you, sir?

Dear Mr. Ravindranath,

We have not communicated for a long time. I assume you are in good health, as I am.

In fact, I am writing this from my daughter's house in New Zealand.

I have spent two months here and tomorrow I will return to Chennai and to Cochin.

In the months of April and May this year, I will be touring the U.S. with my singing group, SING, INDIA.
Please keep us in your prayers.

Remembering the pleasant days of your generous hospitality and affection,
Yours truly,
Jerry Amaldev.

cv Ravindranth

From:	Satish Kumar [s.kumar@qub.ac.uk]
Sent:	Saturday, January 28, 2023 1:26 AM
To:	cv Ravindranth
Subject:	Grandparents

"When an old person dies, a library burns down." This powerful quote reminds us of the immense wealth of knowledge and experience that older generations possess.

It's a tragedy when this knowledge is lost, and it's our responsibility as a society to ensure that it is passed on to future generations.

One way to do this is by incorporating grandparents into our education system.

Allowing grandparents to share their experiences and wisdom in classrooms not only enriches the learning experience for our children, but it also creates an intergenerational bond that benefits both the older and younger generations.

Grandparents have unique perspectives and insights on history, culture, and life lessons that can't be found in textbooks. They have lived through significant events and have valuable insights to share. Imagine the impact of having a grandparent who lived through the Civil Rights movement come into a classroom to talk about their experiences and share their perspectives. This type of learning is invaluable to our children and can help them gain a deeper understanding of the world around them.

Here's 5 ways that including grandparents into your learning environment, will improve your classroom forever:

1. Inviting grandparents to speak in classrooms: Inviting grandparents to come into classrooms and speak about their experiences and perspectives on various topics can add a unique and valuable dimension to the learning experience.

2. Intergenerational mentoring: Pairing grandparents with students in a mentoring capacity can create a positive and mutually beneficial relationship for both parties. The grandparents can share their life experiences, and students can learn from them.

3. Grandparents as volunteer tutors: Grandparents can volunteer as tutors to provide extra help and support to students in the classroom. They can help with homework, reading, and other academic activities.

4. Grandparents as classroom assistants: Grandparents can assist teachers in the classroom by helping with administrative tasks, such as grading papers, and organizing classroom materials.

5. Grandparent-led activities: Encourage grandparents to lead extracurricular activities or clubs that align with their interests and skills, such as knitting, gardening, or cooking. This will give them an opportunity to share their skills and knowledge with students in a fun and engaging way.

Grandparents often feel isolated and disconnected from society, and being involved in their grandchild's education can help to alleviate that feeling. It also helps to create a sense of community and belonging for both the grandparents and the students.

#teachers #education #students #help #learning #opportunity #community #experience #environment #mentoring

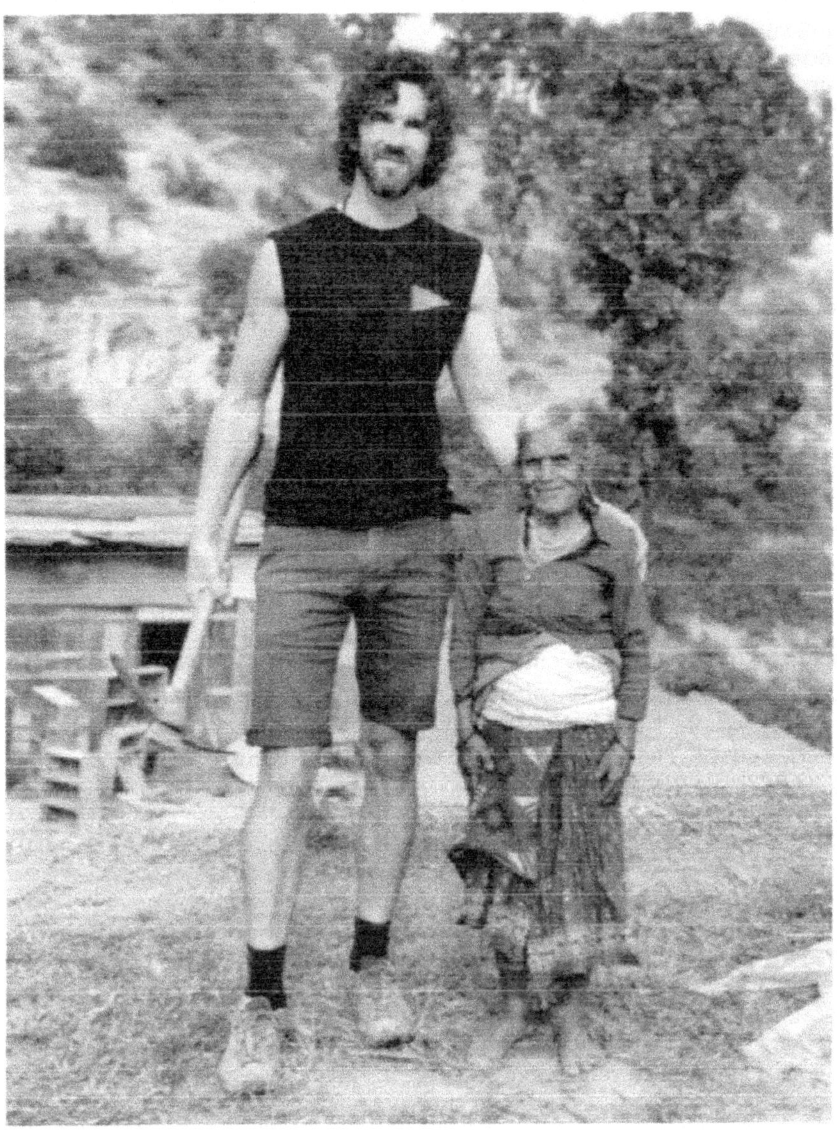

Sent from my iPhone

Dr. M. Satish Kumar, *FRGS, RCS, FHEA*
Faculty of Engineering and Physical Sciences
School of Natural and Built Environment
Research Fellow, *The Senator George J. Mitchell Institute for Global Peace, Security and Justice*
Queen's University Belfast
Belfast BT7 1NN
Northern Ireland, United Kingdom

Tel: +44-(0)28-9097-3479

Distinguished Honorary Chair of Global Sustainable Development Goals (Techno-India University, Kolkata, India, 2023)

Belfast Ambassador's Award, 2020
https://daro.qub.ac.uk/Dr-Satish-Kumar-Belfast-Ambassador-Medal

 Gmail

Ravindranath C.V <sudhacvr@gmail.com>

Greetings from India's First BIS Certified Jeweller.

Rajeev P <kobo@bis.gov.in> Fri, Jun 18, 2021 at 7:06 PM
To: sudhacvr@gmail.com

Thanks. We will try to convey to them.
Congratulations to you also who is the torchbearer of this movement !

With best regards,

राजीव पी Rajeev P वैज्ञानिक एफ एवं प्रमुख Sc F & Head

भारतीय मानक ब्यूरो / Bureau of Indian Standards कोच्चि शाखा कार्यालय / Kochi Branch Office

द्वितीय तल, केंद्रीय भण्डारण निगम क्षेत्रीय कार्यालय परिसर, मावेली रोड, कदवन्त्र, कोच्चि 2nd Floor, Central Warehousing Corporation Regional Office Complex, Maveli Road, Kadavanthra, Kochi.
[Quoted text hidden]

ब्रिगेडियर टी राजेश भानु
कमांडर
Brig T Rajesh Bhanu
Commander
Tele : 6501 (O), 6631 (R)
Mob : 9610033567

GOLDEN JUBILEE YEAR
(1970 - 2020)

51983/TRB/DO

मुख्यालय
५७ पर्वतीय तोपखाना ब्रिगेड
पिन - ९२६९५७
मार्फत ९९ ए पी ओ
Headquarters
57 Mountain Artillery Brigade
PIN - 926957
C/o 99 APO

02 Jan 2021

Dr CV Ravindranath
Managing Partner & Trustee
Krishna Jewels

Respected Maman,

We offer our heartfelt condolences on the demise of our ever-loving 'Ammama'. She was a very special person in our lives too. We will miss her very much. Pl accept our deepest condolences.

Om Shanti

yours sincerely

भारतीय प्रबंध संस्थान कोषिक्कोड
Indian Institute of Management Kozhikode

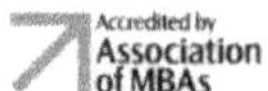

Prof. Debashis Chatterjee
Director

January 23, 2012

Mr. C. V. Ravindranath
Managing Partner
Kunhikannan Jewellery Gold House
Kannur 670 001

Dear Mr. Ravindranath,

I acknowledge with many thanks the receipt of the books that you had very kindly sent to me. I am sure I shall enjoy reading your books.

With warm regards,

Yours sincerely,

(Debashis Chatterjee)

आई.आई.एम.के कॉपस (पोस्ट), कुञ्चमंगलम, कोषिक्कोड – 673 570, केरल, भारत | IIMK Campus (Post), Kunnamangalam, KOZHIKODE – 673 570, Kerala, India
Tele. +91 495 2809200, 2809201 (Direct) **Telefax:** +91 495 2803003 **Fax:** +91 495 2803010 **E-mail:** director@iimk.ac.in **URL:** www.iimk.ac.in/debashis.php

भारतीय प्रबंध संस्थान कोषिक्कोड
Indian Institute of Management Kozhikode

January 12, 2011

Sh. C.V. Ravindranath
Managing Partner
Kunhikannan Jewellery Gold House
Kannur
Kerala – 670 001

Dear Sir,

Sub. : Museum of Indian Business History – Request for Donating   Historical Objects/Artifacts from the Pioneering Leaders of Your Organization to IIM, Kozhikode.

Ref. : Your Letter Dt. 06.12.2010

WISH YOU A VERY HAPPY AND PROSPEROUS NEW YEAR!

This is to thankfully acknowledge the receipt of your letter and copies of documents, which you have so kindly forwarded to us in response to our Director, Prof. Debashis Chatterjee's request for contribution to the Indian Business History Museum, progressing at the IIM Kozhikode.

We wish to assure you that the documents will be preserved in the museum and due acknowledgement will be provided to M/s. Kunnnikannan Jewellery for the kind gesture.

Thanking you for your encouragement.

With kind regards,

Yours faithfully,

Dr. M.G. Sreekumar
Manager, Corporate Communications

BOMBAY HOUSE,
FORT, MUMBAI 400 001.

JANUARY 18, 2008

DEAR MR. RAVINDRANATH,

THANK YOU SO MUCH FOR YOUR LETTER OF JANUARY 11TH AND FOR THE KIND SENTIMENTS YOU HAVE EXPRESSED WHICH I TRULY APPRECIATE.

WITH REGARDS,

YOURS SINCERELY,

RATAN N. TATA

MR. C.V. RAVINDRANATH
KUNHIKANNAN JEWELLERY GOLD HOUSE
KANNUR — 670001
KERALA

June 30, 2006

Ratan N Tata
Chairman

Dear Mr. Ravindranath,

Thank you for your letter of May 26th, and for the kind sentiments you have expressed on the occasion of the recent US-India Business Council award to the House of Tatas.

I greatly appreciate your thoughtful gesture, and your good wishes for the future.

Wishing you well, and with regards,

Yours sincerely,

Ratan N. Tata

Mr. C.V. Ravindranath
Managing Partner
Kunhikannan Jewellery Gold House
Kannur 670 001
Kerala

TATA SONS LIMITED

Bombay House 24 Homi Mody Street Mumbai 400 001
Tel 91 22 204 3725 Fax 91 22 204 2333 e-mail coffice@tata.com

Infosys Technologies Limited
Regd. Office : Plot No. 44, Electronics City
Hosur Road, Bangalore - 561 229, India.
Tel : 91 80 852 0261 Fax : 91 80 852 0362

December 4, 2002

Mr. C. V. Ravindranath,
Managing Partner,
Kunhikannan Jewellery Gold House,
Kannur – 670 001
Telephone: 0497 711025/703375
Facsimile: 0497 767465

Dear Mr. Ravindranath,

Thank you for your letter. I am grateful to you for your kind and encouraging words.

Best regards,

Yours sincerely,

N. R. NARAYANA MURTHY
Chairman and Chief Mentor

HOTEL LEELAVENTURE LIMITED
SAHAR, MUMBAI-400 059 INDIA
Tel.:(91-22)691 12 34. Fax:(91-22)836 73 54.
e-mail:chairman@theleela.com   www.theleela.com

UNITED NATIONS

GLOBAL 500 LAUREATE

C. P. KRISHNAN NAIR
CHAIRMAN

August 5, 2002.

Mr. C.V. Ravindranath
International Chairman
Rotary International Fellowship of Yoga
Managing Partner
Kunhikannan Jewellery Gold House
Kannur – 670001
Kerala.

My dear Ravindranath,

It is better you go to Delhi and see the Minister of Environment personally and bring pressure on him. The son-in-law of M. M. Jacob who is in Madras is a friend of Mr. Balu, you can try to speak to him. Jacob is the Governor of Meghalaya. He is closely known to him. If necessary you can take him alongwith you to get directions to of the Panchayat so that the long delayed project can be activated.

Wishing you all the best in all your endeavors.

With warm regards,

Capt. C.P. Krishnan Nair

THE LEELA PALACE
GOA

A KEMPINSKI HOTEL   Members of
The Leading Hotels of the World

2B, Alexander Square
34/35 Sardar Patel Road
Guindy
Chennai-600 032.
Telephone : 91 (44) 2300083, 2300084
Facsimile : 91 (44) 2300086

Mr. C.V. Ravindranath
Kunhikannan Jewellery Gold House
Bazaar Road
Kannur - 670 001
Kerala.

July 10, 1998

Dear Mr. Ravindranath,

Thanks for your note dated 3/7/98, and I have noted the contents.

Thanks so much for all your letters to me, I am quite impressed by the interest you seem to have to improve the jewellery industry. On my next trip to Calicut I definitely would like to call on you at Cannanore and discuss the ways and means as to how we jointly work together.

Your plans for a jewellery school sounds really interesting. We could discuss further about it in detail when we meet next.

Looking forward to meeting you.

Thanks & regards,

Yours sincerely,

K. SHIVRAM
Manager - South

GURCHARAN DAS
124 Jorbagh
New Delhi 110 003
Tel: 464-8973/463-8061 Fax: 463-2648
E-Mail: gur.das@smb.sprintrpg.ems.vsnl.net.in

Mr. C.V. Ravindranath
Red Sun
Palliyamulla Beach
P.O. Alavil
Kannur - 670 008

February 23, 1998

Dear Ravindranath,

I want to thank you for taking the trouble to respond to my article in the Times of India. I found your suggestions very interesting and valuable. I shall try to incorporate or address your thoughts and concerns in my future columns.

Again, thanks again for writing. Best regards.

Yours,

Gurcharan Das

SHANKAR MENON
Senior Vice-President–Operations
South India Maldives Sri Lanka

November 15, 1997

Mr. C.V. Ravindranath
Managing Director
M. Kunhikannan Jewellery
Azhikode
Kannur – 670 009

Dear Mr. Ravindranath,

This has reference to our Managing Director's letter dated 28th October 1997.

I feel that with the up-gradation of the Kannur Airport, tourists inflow is likely to take place. We have requested the Department of Tourism to give us the development plans for Payyambalam beach so that we can make a feasibility study in relation to the special tourist development area of Bekal.

Thank you once again for recommending our Group to the Hon. Chief Minister of Kerala.

With kind regards,

Yours sincerely,

Shankar Menon

Taj Coromandel, 17, Mahatma Gandhi Road, Chennai-600 034.
Telephone: (044) 827 2827 Telex: (041) 7194 TAJM IN Fax: (044) 825 2502, (044) 825 7104
Registered Office: The Indian Hotels Company Limited, Mandlik House, Mandlik Road, Mumbai 400 001.

Telex:
11- 82442 TAJB IN.
11- 86175 TAJB IN.

Telephone:
(91-22) 202 3366.
Fax: 91-22-2872722

THE INDIAN HOTELS COMPANY LIMITED
The Taj Mahal Hotel, Apollo Bunder, Mumbai - 400 001 India.
Email : Krishnakumar.md.@TajgroupSprintrpg.ems.vsnl.net.in

Managing Director's Office

28 October 1997

Mr. C.V. Ravindranath
Managing Director
M.Kunhikannan Jewellery
Azhikode, Kunnur -670 009
Kerala

Dear Mr. Ravindranath :

Thank you ever so much for your good wishes on my appointment to the Indian Hotels Company Limited.

I have noted with interest your suggestion on the tourism development potential in Kannur. Unfortunately due to my prior commitments I will not be in a position to undertake a personal visit. I am, however, passing on your letter to Mr. Shankar Menon, Vice-President (South) for perusal. As you are probably already aware, the Taj has a joint venture in Kerala with the state tourism department. I am advising Mr. S. Menon to examine whether Kannur fits into the development plans.

I thank you immensely for writing in with your suggestion, and for the interest shown in our group.

Best regards,

Yours sincerely,

(R.K.Krishna Kumar)
Managing Director

cc : Mr. Shankar Menon

Ratan N Tata
Chairman

January 17. 2002

Dear Mr. Ravindranath,

Thank you for your letter of January 12th.

I appreciate your drawing my attention to the proposed development of an international airport at Kannur. However, I need to inform you that the Tata Group's current plans do not envisage investments in the creation of airport infrastructure, and therefore we would not be in a position to respond to your invitation to participate in the Kannur international airport project. Nevertheless, thank you for checking our interest.

With regards,

Yours sincerely,

Ratan N. Tata

Mr. C.V. Ravindranath
President
Rotary Club of Cannanore Seaside
Kunhikannan Jewellary Gold House
Bank Road
Kannur 1
Kerala

TATA INDUSTRIES LIMITED
Bombay House 24 Homi Mody Street Mumbai 400 001
Tel 91 22 204 3725 Fax 91 22 204 2333 e-mail coffice@tata.com

THE LEELA
Kempinski Bombay

THE LEELA BEACH
GOA

C.P. KRISHNAN NAIR
Chairman

July 30, 1994

Mr. C.V. Ravindranath
Managing Partner
Kunhikannan Jewellery
Kannur 670 001
Kerala.

Dear Mr. Ravindranath,

I am in receipt of your letter Ref. CVR 00156/94 dated 16-7-94.

I am pleased to inform you that I shall be in Cannanore from 20th to 25th of August 1994 and would be happy to meet you to discuss the subject matter.

Yours sincerely

Capt. C.P. Krishnan Nair
Chairman

HOTEL LEELAVENTURE LIMITED

Registered Office: The Leela Kempinski Bombay, Sahar, Bombay - 400 059. Tel.: 836 3636 Tlx: 011-79236/79241 KEMP-IN Fax: 836-0606
The Leela Beach Goa, Mobor, Cavelossim Village, Salcette, Goa-403731 Tel: (0834)246363, 246373 Tlx: 0196 268 LELA IN, GOA. Telefax: (0834)246352

Kempinski Hotels are Lufthansa Hotels

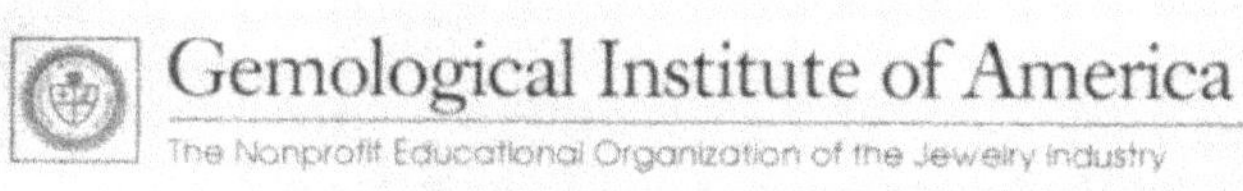

Gemological Institute of America
The Nonprofit Educational Organization of the Jewelry Industry

From the Desk of Wayne Gilcrease, G.G.

August 27, 1991 - FJS-FINAL

C\/Ravindranath 7349335
Colombo House
Cannanore 670001,
KERALA INDIA

Dear C\/.

    What a dynamite way to finish the course--you got 94 percent
on the final and earned your Honors certificate! The drive and
dedication it took to achieve this must be evident in your
performance on the job, too.

    Not only did you get an impressive score on your final AND
earn Honors, but your overall average in the course is 90. That
compares with the current 86 average of your fellow students. Way
to go, C!

    Your Fine Jewelry Sales Honors certificate should arrive in
a couple of weeks if your tuition is paid in full. Otherwise it
will be sent as soon as we receive your final payment.

    Here's what you missed, along with the best answers. I've
noted the page and assignment references so you can look back in
the text to find the logic behind each question.

11. Singles make good customers for fine jewelry because they

A. have higher incomes.
B. buy more jewelry for gifts.
C. have fewer responsibilities.
D. have more disposable income.

The second best answer, D, was your choice, so I am giving you
partial credit, the best answer was C. See Assignment 2, page 7.

22. When customers show interest in a piece, you should first

A. validate their interest.
B. discover their buying motives.
C. point out the piece's qualities.
D. paint a word picture of ownership benefits.

Problems or questions call (800)421-7250, Extension 348

August 27, 1991 - FJS-FINAL
C Ravindranath
Page 2

You chose D, the best answer was A. See Assignment 4, page 4.

Even though you've finished the course you haven't reached the end of your education--you've really just begun. You can expect, with the new information and techniques you've acquired in *Fine Jewelry Sales*, to continue learning more about your customers, and about yourself. As you continue to learn you'll continue to flourish.

There is an additional way to grow as a jewelry professional. As discussed throughout the course material, formal training, and the product knowledge it brings, is the key to lasting success in the jewelry industry.

GIA offers the industry's most widely recognized and respected educational programs. Our *Diamonds* course, for example, is packed with product knowledge and has strengthened the careers of countless jewelry and gemology professionals.

After your performance in this course, especially the hard work it took to earn Honors, you would have no trouble understanding and perfecting your product knowledge. I've enclosed a copy of our course catalog so you can look over our offerings.

Many students have told me they have hesitated to take courses like *Diamonds* because they are afraid it might be too technical. They were pleasantly surprised to discover that, like *Fine Jewelry Sales*, our gemology programs discuss subjects in terms of practical applications. You already have a good idea of what to expect.

Nor should this be the end of our correspondence. I've really enjoyed working with you, C, and genuinely hope you keep in touch. I would especially be interested to hear how well your new skills from this course are serving you.

August 27, 1991 - FJS-FINAL
C Ravindranath
Page 3

Also, if you will call me or write in with your employer's name and address, Dennis Foltz, GIA's Director of Home Study Education, will be happy to write your employer about how well you've done. He won't mention your scores, or the results of your personality profile, but he can describe how well you have done, and point out that you graduated with honors. If you want him to do this for you, please give me your employer's name, the name and address of the business, and your name and student number.

Finally, my sincere congratulations on your accomplishment. I look forward to hearing from you again soon.

Sincerely,

Wayne

SANTHANANDA MUTT
RISHI JNANA SADHANALAYAM TRUST
Reg. No. IV 15/09
Dhyanamala, Kallarakadavu, Pathanamthitta - 689 645, Kerala
Mob: 9061138520

Date: - 26/07/2022

Namaste Dear Blessed Divine Soul Shri Dr.C.V Ravindranath Ji,

I express my heartfelt gratitude for your invitation to 'Shivoham Spiritual Wellness Centre', Kannur. I would like to acknowledge your heartfelt tribute to Sree Sankaracharya by establishment of a nonprofit organization to preserve, protect and promote the non-dualistic philosophy expounded by Sree Adi Sankaracharya.

My due apology in delayed reply as my physical health was not permitting me to do it promptly. Now I am doing well.

I appreciate your selfless work and diligent dedication to preserve the pristine purity of our culture and tradition.

The poetry penned by you depicts as the direct blessings of Sree Sankaracharya and is certain that your heartbeat is reverberating with the All-Pervasive Absolute Truth and Adi Sankaracharya.

Looking forward to join our hands with such organizations like 'Shivoham Spiritual Wellness Centre' with high ideals and noble aim. Request you to pay a visit to our Ashram and Educational institution as per your convenience.

With warm regards and prayers,

Swamini Jnanabha Nishta In The Absolute Truth.

26/07/22.

DEVI JNANABHA NISHTA.
SANTHANANDA MUTT RISHI JNANA SADHANALAYAM
SREE SANTHANANDA VIDYA NIKETHAN.
PATHANAMTHITTA ,KERALA
E-MAIL: swjn123@gmail.com
MOBILE:9061138520

School of Natural and Built Environment
Faculty of Engineering and Physical Sciences
Department of Geography, Archaeology & Palaeoecology
Elmwood Avenue
BELFAST BT7 1 NN
Northern Ireland
Tel: +44 (0)28 9097 3479
Email: s.kumar@qub.ac.uk
www.qub.ac.uk/schools/NBE/

Dr. M. Satish Kumar, *FRGS, RCS, FHEA*
Chairperson, *Kerala Urban Policy Commission*
Fellow, The Senator George J Mitchell Institute for Global Peace, Security and Justice

22 February 2024

Dear Dr. Ravindranath ji

Many Congratulations on this significant Award from your alma mater. It is an honour and pride for all of us who know you.

Your journey has indeed been inspirational and will serve as a guide for future generations too. Your single-minded Commitment to Excellence Dedication and Perseverance is legendary and will be the benchmark like the BIS gold standard that you pioneered.

Wishing you good health, prosperity and a long life

Yours truly

Dr. M. Satish Kumar & Nuala McCarthy

CHAPTER V

ECONOMIC GROWTH

We need the support of Local, State and Central Governments to create wealth for our birth land and Mother Country, for the welfare of our brothers and sisters living in our society.

29 letters of Hope for the Economic Growth of India from 12.6.1972 to 6.11.2023

കേരള സർക്കാർ

പിണറായി വിജയൻ
കേരള മുഖ്യമന്ത്രി

06.11.2023

പ്രിയ സുഹൃത്തേ,

ക്ഷേമവും വികസനവും ലക്ഷ്യമിട്ടുള്ള യാത്രയിൽ കേരളം രാജ്യത്തിന് മാതൃകയായി മുന്നിൽ നിൽക്കുകയാണ്. ലക്ഷക്കണക്കിനാളുകൾക്കു വീടുണ്ടാക്കിയും സ്കൂളുകൾ മുതൽ ആതുരാലയങ്ങൾ വരെ അത്യാധുനിക സൗകര്യങ്ങളോടുകൂടിയതാക്കിയും റോഡുകളും പാലങ്ങളും മെച്ചപ്പെടുത്തിയും അതിദാരിദ്ര്യം ഇല്ലാതാക്കിയും കുട്ടികൾക്കു പഠനസാമഗ്രികൾ കൃത്യസമയത്തു ലഭ്യമാക്കിയും നമ്മുടെ നാട് മുന്നേറുകയാണ്. മത നിരപേക്ഷതയും സൗഹാർദവും സമാധാനാന്തരീക്ഷവും ഉറപ്പുവരുത്തിക്കൊണ്ട് പുരോഗതിയിലേക്ക് നീങ്ങുന്ന സമൂഹവും നാടുമാണ് നമ്മുടേത്.

തുടർച്ചയായി തടസ്സവാദങ്ങളും സാമ്പത്തിക വൈതരണികളുമുണ്ടായി. ഉപരോധ സമാനമായ സമീപനങ്ങളുണ്ടാകുന്നു. നമ്മുടെ നേട്ടങ്ങൾ ചൂണ്ടിക്കാട്ടി നമുക്കുള്ള അവകാശങ്ങൾ നിഷേധിക്കപ്പെടുന്ന സ്ഥിതി ഉണ്ടാകുന്നു. എന്നാൽ അടങ്ങാത്ത ഇച്ഛാശക്തിയോടെ നീങ്ങിയാൽ ഒന്നും ഒന്നിനും തടസ്സമല്ല എന്നുറപ്പാക്കിക്കൊണ്ട് പുതിയ വഴികൾ വെട്ടി നാം മുന്നേറി. ആ മുന്നേറ്റത്തിന്റെ അടുത്ത ഘട്ടം എങ്ങനെയാവണം? അത് അധികാര കേന്ദ്രങ്ങളല്ല, ജനമനസ്സുകളാണു നിശ്രയിക്കേണ്ടത്. ജനങ്ങളുടെ നാഡിമിടിപ്പറിഞ്ഞേ ഈ സർക്കാർ പ്രവർത്തിക്കൂ.

ഈ ചിന്തയോടെ ഓരോ നിയോജക മണ്ഡലത്തിലും **നവകേരള സദസ്സ്** സംഘടിപ്പിക്കുകയാണ്. നവംബർ 18ന് മഞ്ചേശ്വരത്ത് ആരംഭിച്ച് ഡിസംബർ 24ന് തിരുവനന്തപുരത്ത് സമാപിക്കും.

ജനാധിപത്യത്തിന്റെ ക്രിയാത്മകവും പ്രായോഗികവുമായ തലങ്ങൾ സാർഥകമാക്കുന്ന ഈ വിപുലമായ പരിപാടിയിൽ മുഖ്യമന്ത്രിയും മന്ത്രിമാരാകെയും പങ്കെടുക്കും. ജനകീയ പ്രശ്നങ്ങൾ പരിഹരിക്കാൻ താലൂക്ക് തല അദാലത്തുകൾ മുതൽ മേഖലാ അവലോകന യോഗങ്ങൾ വരെ പൂർത്തിയാക്കിയതിന്റെ അടുത്ത ഘട്ടം കൂടിയാണ് ഈ നിയോജക മണ്ഡലതല ബഹുജന സദസ്സ്.

ഈ സദസ്സിനു മുന്നോടിയായി **2023 നവംബർ 21** ചൊവ്വാഴ്ച രാവിലെ ഒൻപതു മണിക്ക് **കണ്ണൂർ ബർണശ്ശേരിയിലെ ഇ.കെ. നായനാർ അക്കാദമിയിൽ** വെച്ച് നടക്കുന്ന പ്രഭാത ഭക്ഷണ കൂടിച്ചേരലിലേക്ക് മുഖ്യമന്ത്രിയോടും മന്ത്രിമാരോടും സംവദിക്കുന്നതിനായി സമൂഹത്തിലെ സവിശേഷ ഇടപെടൽ നടത്തുന്ന വ്യക്തി എന്ന നിലയിൽ താങ്കളുടെ സാന്നിധ്യം ക്ഷണിക്കുകയാണ്. ഉറപ്പായും എത്തിച്ചേരാനും നിർദ്ദേശങ്ങൾ മുമ്പോട്ടുവെക്കാനും അഭ്യർത്ഥിക്കുന്നു.

സ്നേഹപൂർവ്വം,

പിണറായി വിജയൻ

(Registered Under Societies Registration Act XXI of 1860)

ECONOMIC GROWTH FOUNDATION

115, Ist Floor, Vardhman Mayur Market, Near MIG Pocket-6, Mayur Vihar Phase-3, Delhi - 110096.
Mob: 9818490219, 7303933154, E-mail: economicgrowth60@gmail.com, Web: www.economicgrowth.in

EGF/AEBGJ/023/ 13th April`2023
11th January` 2023

TO
DR. C.V. RAVINDRANATH
KANNUR-

Sub: "AWARD FOR EXCELLENCE IN BEST GEM & JEWELLER"

Dear Sir/Madam,

We are pleased to inform that your name has been Selected to receive the **"AWARD FOR EXCELLENCE IN BEST GEM & JEWELLER"** for your outstanding achievements and contributions in your field of activities by the Selection committee in view of your Bio-data. The Award presentation ceremony Will be held on **13th April 2023 at New Delhi**

We are sending you the Selection letter along with Participant Form. You are requested to fill up the form with one photographs affixed on the form with Participant fees drawn in Favour of **"ECONOMIC GROWTH FOUNDATION"** by Courier/Speed Post. Your document should reach to us latest by **05-02-2023.** Function is followed by Hi-Tea. If you are not able to receive the Award personally, under any unforeseen circumstances, the Award will be sent to you by **Courier/Speed Post,** after receiving your reply, we will send the Invitation card along with the programme details.

Once again, **"Heartiest Congratulations"** for this Prestigious Award.
Your earliest response will be highly appreciated.

With warm regards
For E.G.F.

Jeet Singh
Gen. Secretary

കമ്മ്യൂണിസ്റ്റ് പാർടി ഓഫ് ഇന്ത്യ (മാർക്സിസ്റ്റ്)
കേരള സംസ്ഥാന കമ്മിറ്റി

Phone : 0471-2305731, 2305733
Fax : 2307141
E-mail : akgcentre@gmail.com
എ.കെ.ജി. സെന്റർ
തിരുവനന്തപുരം - 695 034.

04.09.2022

ഡോ. സി.വി.രവീന്ദ്രനാഥ്
ജവഹർ റോഡ്, താവക്കര
കണ്ണൂർ, 670001

പ്രീയ സുഹൃത്തെ,

അഭിനന്ദനം അറിയിച്ചതിൽ അതിയായ സന്തോഷം. ടൂറിസം വികസനവുമായി ബന്ധപ്പെട്ട താങ്കളുടെ നിർദ്ദേ ശങ്ങൾ പാർടി പരിശോധിക്കുന്നതാണ്.

അഭിവാദ്യങ്ങളോടെ,

സെക്രട്ടറി

KANNUR DASARA

Organised by:

MUNICIPAL CORPORATION OF KANNUR
കണ്ണൂർ മുനിസിപ്പൽ കോർപ്പറേഷൻ

Municipal Corporation Office, PB No. 39, Kannur, Kerala - 670 001
Tel: 0497 2700142, 91889 55288
E-mail: kannurmunicipalcorporation@gmail.com

Chairman, Organising Committee
Adv. T.O. Mohanan (Mayor, Kannur Corporation)
Tel: 94470 30403, 91889 55288

Gen. Convener, Organising Committee
K.C. Rajan Master
Tel: 9447 883346

മാനേജർ
M/s. കൃഷ്ണ ജുവലേഴ്സ്
താവക്കര, കണ്ണൂർ

നീണ്ട ഇടവേളക്കു ശേഷം 2022 സെപ്തംബർ 26 മുതൽ ഒക്ടോബർ 4 വരെ ഒൻപത് ദിവസങ്ങളിലായി കണ്ണൂർ കലക്ട്രേറ്റ് മൈതാനിയിൽ കണ്ണൂർ കോർപ്പറേഷൻ സംഘടിപ്പിച്ച 'കണ്ണൂർ ദസറ'യുടെ വിജയത്തിൽ താങ്കളും താങ്കളുടെ സ്ഥാപനവും വഹിച്ച പങ്ക് കേവലമായ നന്ദിവാക്കുകൾക്കതീതമാണ്.

കോവിഡിന്റെ പേടിപ്പെടുത്തുന്ന അടച്ചിടലുകൾക്കും, അകലം പാലിക്കലിനും ശേഷം അടുത്തിടപഴകാനും ഒത്തുചേർന്ന് ആഘോഷങ്ങൾ നടത്തുന്നതിനും കൈവന്ന സുവർണ്ണാവസരമായിരുന്നു 'കണ്ണൂർ ദസറ'. ആഘോഷം എന്നതിൽ ഉപരി നമ്മുടെ സമൂഹം നേരിടുന്ന ലഹരി എന്ന മാരക വിപത്തിനെതിരെയുള്ള പോരാട്ടം കൂടിയാക്കി മാറ്റുന്നതിനും 'കണ്ണൂർ ദസറ'ക്ക് സാധിച്ചു, എന്നതിൽ നമുക്ക് അഭിമാനിക്കാം. അതോടൊപ്പം നഗരത്തിലെ വ്യാപാര മേഖലയ്ക്ക് പുത്തനുണർവ്വ് നൽകുന്നതിനും 'കണ്ണൂർ ദസറ'യിലൂടെ സാധിച്ചു എന്നതും പ്രസക്തമാണ്.

ഇതെല്ലാം സാധിച്ചത് താങ്കളെപ്പോലുള്ളവരുടെ നിസ്സീമമായ സഹായ സഹകരണങ്ങൾ കൊണ്ടു മാത്രമാണ്. താങ്കളുടെ സഹകരണത്തിന് നന്ദി രേഖപ്പെടുത്തുന്നതോടൊപ്പം ഭാവിയിൽ കോർപ്പറേഷൻ സംഘടിപ്പിക്കുന്ന എല്ലാ സദുദ്യമങ്ങൾക്കും സഹകരണവും പിന്തുണയും ഉണ്ടാകണമെന്ന് അഭ്യർത്ഥിക്കുന്നു.

സ്നേഹപൂർവ്വം,

അഡ്വ.ടി.ഒ മോഹനൻ
മേയർ
കണ്ണൂർ മുനിസിപ്പൽ കോർപ്പറേഷൻ
Adv. T.O. MOHANAN
Mayor
Kannur Municipal Corporation

കണ്ണൂർ
11–10–2022

cv Ravindranth

From:	Kirankumar Kannur AirPort [kirankumar@kannurairport.aero]
Sent:	Thursday, June 22, 2023 1:09 PM
To:	Ravindranath C.V
Cc:	MD Kannur Airport; usad-moca@gov.in; Krishna Kumar Singh; us-ir.sb@gov.in
Subject:	Fw: Ministry of Civil Aviation - Reply Letter
Attachments:	Airport Privatization.pdf

Dear Dr. C.V Ravindranath,

Greetings from Kannur International Airport !!!

Reference is invited to the attached letter (Regn. No. PMOPG/E/2023/0080032) from Ministry of Civil Aviation.

Please be informed that Kannur International Airport is always eager to promote local flavors related to culture, art, architecture, cuisine, etc. We would like to mention that our Terminal building boasts with paintings & art forms (of local folklore, theyyam, kalaripayattu, Ayurveda ... etc.), details provided as under.

Sl. No.	Art work item	Location
1	Theyyam	Arrival Immigration
2	Metal art work - Thalakavery	International SHA
3	Ancient Payyanur Bazar – Acrylic Art work	Domestic SHA
4	Kerala Art forms(Mural Art work)	International Departure Security Check
5	Festivals of Kerala -Mural Art work	International Remote SHA
6	Heritage of Malabar (Acrylic Mural works)	International Remote SHA
7	Yakshagana (Mural Art work)	International SHA ramp.
8	Ayurveda (Cement Relief)	International Arrival
9	Circus -Cement Relief art work	International Arrival
10	Ayurveda - Terracotta art work	Domestic Arrival
11	Kalari payattu- Metal art work	Arrival Hall and International Security check area.

In addition we have tourism counters at both domestic & international arrival halls, and purportedly tourism department has quite actively put Kannur Airport in its priority lists.

We thank you for being a well-wisher of Kannur International Airport.

With Regards,

K. Kiran Kumar,
MANAGER - AIRPORT OPERATIONS,
Kannur International Airport Ltd,

Kannur International Airport (P.O), Mattanur, Kannur, Kerala, India, 670708.
+91- 9847614799 (Mobile)
www.kannurairport.in

From: Dhanya Kannurairport <dhanya@kannurairport.aero>
Sent: Thursday, June 22, 2023 11:37 AM
To: Kirankumar Kannur AirPort <kirankumar@kannurairport.aero>
Subject: Fw: Ministry of Civil Aviation - Reply Letter

Dear Kiran,

As informed by MD, please see attached letter for necessary action.

Thanks

Dhanya N Sunil
EA to MD/AM
Kannur International Airport Limited
Mattannur
Kannur, Kerala - 670 708
Tel: 0490 2481000
www.kannurairport.aero

From: MD Kannur Airport <md@kannurairport.aero>
Sent: Thursday, June 22, 2023 11:34 AM
To: Dhanya Kannurairport <dhanya@kannurairport.aero>
Subject: Fw: Ministry of Civil Aviation - Reply Letter

Dinesh Kumar.C
Managing Director,
Kannur International Airport Limited
Mattannur
Kannur, Kerala - 670 708
Tel: 0490 2481000
www.kannurairport.aero

From: Ravindranath C.V <sudhacvr@gmail.com>
Sent: Thursday, June 22, 2023 10:34 AM
To: MD Kannur Airport <md@kannurairport.aero>; Info Kannurairport <info@kannurairport.aero>
Subject: Ministry of Civil Aviation - Reply Letter

DR.. C. V. RAVINDRANATH
MANAGING PARTNER
KRISHNA JEWELS
JAWAHAR ROAD

cv Ravindranth

From:	Kirankumar Kannur AirPort [kirankumar@kannurairport.aero]
Sent:	Monday, June 26, 2023 11:27 AM
To:	Ravindranath C.V
Subject:	Fw: AIRPORT PRIVATIZATION.pdf
Attachments:	PMOPG D 2022 0263316.pdf; NHAI dt. 13.12.2022.pdf; US Petition RB dt 18-11-2022.pdf

Respected Sir,

Greetings from Kannur International Airport!!!

We thank for the great support extended towards betterment of Kannur International Airport and for projecting true potential of North Malabar region.

KIAL management also constantly apprising central government for awarding point of call status to kannur airport in order to get foreign carriers on board.

Obtaining point of call status will be a significant step towards attracting foreign carriers and expanding international connectivity. It would not only facilitate easier travel for passengers but also contribute to the economic growth of the region. By constantly apprising the central government about this matter, the management is actively working towards achieving this goal.

We once again thank for your continued support.

With Regards,

K. Kiran Kumar,
MANAGER - AIRPORT OPERATIONS,
Kannur International Airport Ltd,
Kannur International Airport (P.O), Mattanur, Kannur, Kerala, India, 670708.
+91- 9847614799 (Mobile)
www.kannurairport.in

AAI/CHQ/JVC/PPP-II/2023/   Date: 12.04.2023

Shri Dr. C V Ravindranath,
Krishna Jewels Jawahar Road,
Thavakkara Jawahar Road, Thavakkara
Kannur, Kerala
7558888336,
sudhacvr@gmail.com

Sub :- **All Indian Airports must be given to Private Companies to operate especially Adani Airports to maintain International Standard.**

Dear Sir,

This has reference to your letter dated 25.03.2023 addressed to Hon'ble Prime Minister, Government of India requesting for All Indian Airports must be given to Private Companies to operate especially Adani Airports to maintain International Standard.

Sl. No.	Query	Comments
1	Since America, Europe and China have become unsafe to travel, Indian Tourism will be increased by 39.5% in 2023-2024. By 2025, India will have 225 Airports with an Investment of Rs. 98,000 Crores. The Income of Airport operators in India will have an increment of 26 % with a turnover of Rs. Rs.32,390/= So, it is highly essential that all the Airports in India, must be operated by private companies to increase our Tourists to 40 crores per year. State Govts. must not do business, they must only govern, so that corruption could be curbed in govt. machineries and Ministers. Adani Airports must be given many airports in India, because they can develop it to International Standards. They have the experience and expertise in running huge airports in India. By 2023, 9 crores travelers	As per the National Monetization Pipeline (NMP) of Govt of India, twenty-five (25) airports have been identified for monetization over FY 2022-25. The NMP provides for monetization of following airports as per phasing specified below: (table below)

S.No.	Name of Airport	S.No.	Name of Airport
6 Airports in FY22		6 Airports in FY24	
1	Bhubaneswar	1	Chennai
2.	Varanasi	2	Vijayawada
3.	Amritsar	3	Tirupati
4.	Trichy	4	Vadodara
5.	Indore	5	Bhopal
6.	Raipur	6	Hubballi
8 Airports in FY 23		5 Airports in FY25	
1	Calicut	1	Imphal
2	Coimbatore	2	Agartala
3	Nagpur*	3	Udaipur
4	Patna	4	Dehradun
5	Madurai	5	Rajahmundry
6	Surat		
7	Ranchi		
8	Jodhpur		

must be managed in such Airports to take Indian Tourism to the highest peak of world Tourism. India had got high potential in Air of Travel under your leadership of your excellence.	AAI Board has recommended clubbing/pairing of 05 (five) select Airports with 06 (six) small Airports for leasing-out under PPP mode for Operations, Management and Development as under.

Group	Select Airport	Small Airport (s)
1.	Amritsar (Punjab)	Kangra (Gaggal) (HP)
2.	Varanasi (U.P.)	Kushinagar (UP) and Gaya (Bihar)
3.	Bhubaneshwar (Odisha)	Hubballi (Karnataka)
4.	Raipur (Chhattisgarh)	Aurangabad (Maharashtra)
5..	Trichy (T.N.)	Tirupati (A.P.)

The proposal has been submitted to MoCA for obtaining in-principle approval of Union Cabinet, which is awaited.

PPP transaction of the above-mentioned airports shall be as per the directives of Government. of India.

Thanking you,

Yours faithfully,

(N.V. Subbarayudu)
Executive Director-II (JVC/PPP)

Ravindranath C.V <sudhacvr@gmail.com>

PMOPG/E/2023/045651 and PMOPG/E/2022/00333012 - Bharat Seacoast Express Highway - - Reg.

NHAI RO Chennai <nhaichennairo@gmail.com>   Sat, Apr 1, 2023 at 3:11 PM
To: ravinder@nhai.org
Cc: sudhacvr@gmail.com

To
GM(Bharatmala), NHAI HQ, New Delhi

Sir,
Please find enclosed herewith the CPGRAMS received requesting for Bharat Seacoast Express Highway connecting Gujarat, Maharashtra, Goa, Karnataka, Kerala, Pondicherry, Tamil Nadu, Andhra Pradesh and Odisha and Bengal. It is requested to examine the PG and furnish reply to the petitioner directly with a copy to this office.
Regards
DGM(T)
National Highways Authority of India
Regional Office - Chennai
SRI Tower, 3rd Floor
DP - 34 (SP), Industrial Estate,
Guindy, Chennai-600 032.
Phone No: 044 - 22252635
Fax No: 044 - 22252636

⚤▲Print this mail only if absolutely necessary. Save Paper.Save Trees.

4 attachments

pmopg 045651 24.02.2023.pdf
71K

pmopg 0333012.pdf
72K

pmopg 0333012 encl.pdf
969K

pmopg encl 045651.pdf
1191K

Details for registration number : PMOPG/E/2023/0045651

Name   DR C V Ravindranath

Date of receipt   24/02/2023

Address   Krishna Jewels Thavakkara Jawahar Road

District name   Kannur

State name   Kerala

Mobile no   7558888336

Email Id   sudhacvr@gmail.com

Grievance description

Road Transport and Highways >> Suggestions/Miscellaneous/Others >> Others

Ministry/Organisation : Ministry of Road Transport and Highways (MORTH)
Policies/Act/Rules related which suggestions is furnished : Bharath Seacoast Express Highway

----

Shri Narendra Modi,
Hon. Prime Minister of India

Respected Sir,

Sub : Bharath Seacoast Express Highway connecting 1. Gujarat, 2. Maharastra, 3. Goa,
4. Karnataka, 5. Kerala, 6. Pondicherry, 7. Tamil Nadu, 8. Andhra Pradesh,
9. Odisha and Bengal.

Hare Krishna!

Please find the attached document Bharath Seacoast Express Highway.

Krishna Bless!
Very Truly Yours,

DR. C.V. Ravindranath HMCT, PDSHM, MA, MPhil, PhD (Mgmt) , PhD (Philo), D.Litt(SQ)
Tantric SQ Research Student
Alumni : IIM-A, IHM-M, ISB-H, GIA-USA

22.2.2023

Name of organisation(s) where grievance is pending   1. NHAI RO Chennai

Type of receipt   Takenup

[🖶 Print] [✖ Close]

Patrons

Pinarayi Vijayan
(Chief Minister)

P. Rajeev
(Minister for Law,
Industries and Coir)

M.B. Rajesh
(Minister for
Local Self Governments)

**Adv. P.A.
Mohamed Riyas**
(Minister for Tourism)

A. N. Shamseer
(Speaker, Kerala
Legislative Assembly)

**Ramachandran
Kadannappalli**
(MLA, Kannur)

Arun K Vijayan IAS
(Collector, Kannur District)

Chairman
P.P. Divya
(President,
Kannur District Panchayat)

General Convener
A.S. Shiras
(General Manager,
District Industries Centre)

Convener
A.V. Abdul Latheef
(Secretary,
Kannur District Panchayat)

Convener
P.V. Ravindra Kumar
Manager (District Panchayat)
District Industries Centre, Kannur

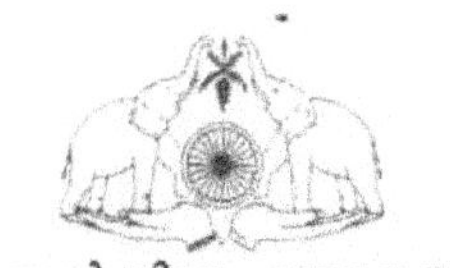

കണ്ണൂർ ജില്ലാ പഞ്ചായത്ത്

📞 0497 2700306, +91 8593 958 881 ✉ dpknnr@gmail.com, kannurdpinvestorsdesk@gmail.com

To,

Dr .Shri .C.V.Raveendranath
Chairman
Krishna Beach Resort

Dear Sir,

The NRI INVESTORS SUMMIT, hosted by Kannur District Panchayat, is a distinguished two-day event, taking place on October 30th and 31st, 2023. This summit features a unique theme, with the first day dedicated to Industries & Agriculture, and the second day focusing on Tourism, Hospitality & Wellness. The esteemed inauguration of this event is set for 10 am on October 30th, 2023, with the Hon'ble Minister, Shri P. Rajive, presiding over the proceedings, holding portfolios of Industries & Law.

It is with great pleasure and anticipation that I extend this invitation to you on behalf of the organizing committee for the NRI INVESTORS SUMMIT, specifically regarding a significant Tourism-related meeting and discussion scheduled for October 31st, 2023.

We recognize and deeply appreciate your invaluable contributions to the tourism sector, exemplified by your role as Chairman of Krishna Beach Resort. It is our honor to invite you to be a part of the discussions and deliberations that will shape the future of tourism, hospitality, and wellness.

The Tourism-related meeting on October 31st, 2023, will provide an ideal platform to share your insights and experiences, as well as explore collaborative opportunities with fellow industry leaders and experts.

For any inquiries or further information about this event, please do not hesitate to contact Mr. Subhash at 9846113263. Your presence and contributions would be instrumental in making this meeting a remarkable success.

Thank you for considering our invitation, and we look forward to your participation on October 31st, 2023, at the NRI INVESTORS SUMMIT.

Warm regards
Smt.P.P.Divya
President, Kannur District Panchayath

P. K. SREEMATHI TEACHER
MINISTER FOR HEALTH & SOCIAL WELFARE

Phone {
Office : 0471- 2333833
       2335266
Res : 0471- 2319037
       2319042
Fax : 2335266
e-mail-pksreemathy@yahoo.com

GOVERNMENT SECRETARIAT
THIRUVANANTHAPURAM

DATE : ....
27.9.2006

Dear Shri Ravindranath,

Thank you for your letter congratulating me on my winning State Assembly Election and also for your valuable suggestions for the development of North Malabar. I am bringing your suggestions to the notice of the concerned Ministers for urgent necessary action in respect of those requests. Such suggestions from your side in future will always be welcomed and I assure you that I shall try my level best in getting the possible demands cherished.

With regards,

Yours sincerely,

P.K. SREEMATHI TEACHER

Shri C.V. Ravindranath,
Managing Partner,
Kunhikannan Jewellery Gold House,
Kannur – 670 001.

L. K. Advani
President

Bharatiya Janata Party

Dated: November 22, 2004

Dear Friend,

Thank you very much for your greetings on my nomination as National President of Bharatiya Janata Party.

May God give me strength to measure up to the expectations of all friends and well wishers like you.

With regards,

Yours sincerely,

(L.K. Advani)

Shri C.V. Ravindranath,
Kunhikannam Jewellery Gold House,
Kannur-670 001,
Kerala

एम. वेंकैया नायडू ,सांसद
अध्यक्ष
M. Venkaiah Naidu, MP
President

Nation First, Party Next and Self Last

भारतीय जनता पार्टी
Bharatiya Janata Party

February 22, 2003

Dear Shri Ravindranath,

Namasthe,

I was happy to receive your book of poems 'My Love Unto Thee'. The merit of these poems is apparent at first glance and I am looking forward to going through them at leisure.

Yours sincerely,

(M. Venkaiah Naidu)

Shri C. V. Ravindranath,
Red Sun,
Palliyamulla Beach,
P.O. Alavil,
Kannur – 670 008
(Kerala)

11, Ashok Road, New Delhi - 110 001, Tel : 23782604, 23382234, 23382235, Fax : 23782163

30, Aurangazeb Road, New Delhi-110 011, Tel : 23794080, 23019388, Fax : 23019387

K. SUDHAKARAN

MINISTER FOR FORESTS & SPORTS

PHONE ⎧ OFFICE: 327039
　　　　　　　　　　327295
　　　　⎩ RES: 312326
　　　　　　　　　313295

THIRUVANANTHAPURAM

DATE...... 12-09-2002.

No. 5061/K5/2002/M/ (F &S)

Dear Shri. Ravindranath,

Thank you for your letter of 15 th August, 2002. I am much impressed by your devotion to humanity and sincerely hope for your continued co- operation.

With regards,

K. SUDHAKARAN

Rtn.PHF C.V. Ravindranath.

Managing Partner,

M/s Kunhikannan Jewellery Gold House,

Kannur 670001.

Dr. D. BABU PAUL

ADDITIONAL CHIEF SECRETARY

TEL. { OFFICE: 327421 / 468805 RES: 316631

GOVERNMENT OF KERALA
THIRUVANANTHAPURAM

22.7.1998

My dear *Ravindranath Avl.,*
Namaskaram

This acknowledges your letter dated 14.7.98.
I have passed it on to the Director of Technical
Education. You may also like to contact Shri.P.N.
Suresh, Executive Officer, Vasthu Vidhya Gurukulam,
Arammula, Pathanamthitta Dist. This is a Government
Society chaired by me, devoted to traditional
architecture, mural art etc. Perhaps independent
of the University we can start a course in the
Gurukulam.

Yours *sincerely,*

Shri.C.V.Ravindranath,
Managing Partner,
Kunhikannan Jewellery Gold House,
Kannur-670 001.

श्री लालकृष्ण आडवाणी

अध्यक्ष, भाजपा संसदीय दल का कार्यालय

Office of Shri L.K. Advani

Chairman, BJP Parliamentary Party

Dated: June 13, 2012

Shri C.V. Ravindranath,
Kunhikannan Jewellery Gold House,
Kannur – 670 001
Kerala State.

Dear Sir,

I am desired to acknowledge receipt and thank you for your letter dated 7th June, 2012 regarding political crimes in Ker4ala.

Your letter has been put up to Shri L.K. Advani ji for his kind perusal.

With regards,

Yours sincerely,

(DEEPAK CHOPRA)
SECRETARY

30, पृथ्वीराज रोड, नई दिल्ली-110 011 दूरभाष : 23794124, 23794125 फैक्स : 23013142
30, Prithviraj Road, New Delhi-110 011 Tel : 23794124, 23794125 Fax : 23013142

सत्यमेव जयते

रक्षा मंत्री
भारत
MINISTER OF DEFENCE
INDIA

D. O. No. 25191 RM/2012

09 June, 2012

Dear Shri C.V. Ravindranath,

I am in receipt of your letter dated 28th May, 2012 regarding tracking of political crimes in Kerala. I have noted the contents of the letter.

With regards,

Yours sincerely,

(A.K. Antony)

Shri C.V. Ravindranath
Kunhikannan Jewellery Gold House
Kannur, Kerala – 670 001

Office : 104, South Block, New Delhi-110011. Ph. : 23012286, 23019030 Fax : 23015403
Resi. : 9, Krishna Menon Marg, New Delhi - 110011. Ph. : 23013611. Fax : 23013612

D. O. No. 1941 RM/2012

04 May, 2012

Dear Shri C.V. Ravindranath,

I am in receipt of your letter dated 26th April, 2012 regarding train quota for students attending interviews to pursue higher studies and research.

With regards,

Yours sincerely,

(A.K. Antony)

Shri C.V. Ravindranath
Kunhikannan Jewellery Gold House
Kannur, Kerala -- 670 001

Office : 104, South Block, New Delhi-110011, Ph. : 23012286, 23019030 Fax : 23015403
Resi. : 9, Krishna Menon Marg, New Delhi - 110011, Ph. : 23013611, Fax : 23013612

सत्यमेव जयते

रक्षा मंत्री
भारत
**MINISTER OF DEFENCE
INDIA**

D. O. No. 1077 RM/2012

15 March, 2012

Dear Shri C.V. Ravindranath,

I am in receipt of your letter dated 24th January, 2012 regarding shifting of Territorial Army and DSC from Kannur Fort Maidan. I have noted the contents of the letter.

With regards,

Yours sincerely,

(A.K. Antony)

Shri C.V. Ravindranath
Kunhikannan Jewellery Gold House
Kannur, Kerala – 670 001

Office : 104, South Block, New Delhi-110011, Ph. : 23012286, 23019030 Fax : 23015403
Resi. : 9, Krishna Menon Marg, New Delhi - 110011, Ph. : 23013611, Fax : 23013612

अध्यक्ष, लोक सभा
SPEAKER, LOK SABHA

New Delhi
31 July 2008

Dear Shri Ravindranath,

I thank you very much for your gracious letter and like to convey my deepest appreciation to you for your support, which I shall always cherish.

The unprecedented, overwhelming and positive response that I have received from you and other like-minded persons, from different parts of India and overseas is essentially the manifestation of a strong desire to see high standards of performance being set by people's representatives and for restoration of the dignity of Parliament.

Your good wishes have, no doubt, given me the enhanced encouragement to carry forward the challenging task of upholding the principles enshrined in the Constitution.

I believe that the people generally and particularly the political parties should ensure that the potential of our democratic system is more meaningful harnessed to fulfil the aspirations and needs of the people of our great country.

With best wishes,

Yours sincerely,

(Somnath Chatterjee)

Shri C.V. Ravindranath,
Kunhikannan Jewellery Gold House,
Kannur – 670 001, Kerala.

L. K. ADVANI
LEADER OF OPPOSITION
(LOK SABHA)

44, PARLIAMENT HOUSE
NEW DELHI - 110 001
PHONE : 23016705, 23034285
FAX : 23017470

August 4, 2004

MESSAGE

I am happy to know that Kunhikannan Jewellery Gold House, Kannur is bringing out its maiden newsletter, "Mayyilpilli" to impart knowledge among the consumers about the purity and quality of gold.

I congratulate the staff and management of the Gold House on this occasion and wish them all success in their endeavour.

(L.K. Advani)

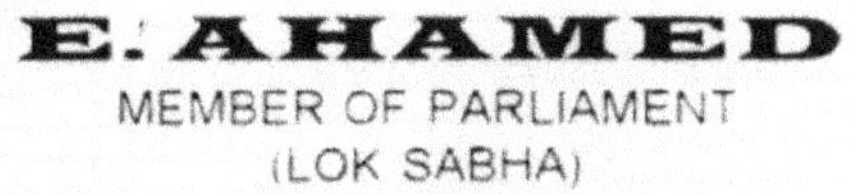

E. AHAMED
MEMBER OF PARLIAMENT
(LOK SABHA)

18, FEROZE SHAH ROAD,
NEW DELHI - 110 001
PHONE : 011-3711424
TELEFAX : 011-3351463
e-mail : eahamed@hotmail.com
eahmed@sansad-nic.in

Dated the 22nd August, 2002.

Dear Rtn C. V. Ravindranath,

Thank you very much for your letter dated 10th August, 2002 regarding a proposal for an airport in Kannur. I agree with you that there is a need for an airport in Kannur and all of us must strive our very best to have it.

It is true that we have three airports in Kerala at Thiruvananthapuram, Ernakulam and Calicut. But Calicut airport has not yet been declared as an international airport despite the fact that there are about 3 dozen overseas flights operating from Calicut. I am, as a Member of Parliament representing that area, trying my very best to get the Calicut airport declared as an international airport. I appreciate the sentiments of people of Kannur and I shall also try to do my best in this matter.

Thanking you,

Yours sincerely,

(E. AHAMED)

Rtn. PHF C.V. Ravindranath
Managing Partner,
Kunhikannan Jewellery Gold House,
Kannur-670 001 (Kerala)

E. AHAMED

MEMBER OF PARLIAMENT
(LOK SABHA)

18, FEROZE SHAH ROAD
NEW DELHI-110 001.
TEL. : 011-3711424
TELEFAX : 011-3351463
email : eahamed@hotmail.com
eahmed@sansad.nic.in

12 February 2002

Dear Shri Ravindranath,

I have received your letter dated 9th January 2002 informing me about the formation of North Malabar Development Board under the auspices of Rotary Club of Cannanore Seaside. Since I was out of the country, I could not acknowledge the receipt of your letter. Please excuse me for the same.

I wish all success to all the endeavours of the Board regarding the development of the North Malabar Region. I shall be only happy to extend whatever support I will be able to.

With you all success, with warm regards,

Yours sincerely,

E. AHAMED

Shri C.V. Ravindranath
President, Rotary Club of Cannanore Seaside
Kunhikannan Jewellery Gold House
Bank Road, Kannur-1
Kerala

वसुन्धरा राजे

Vasundhara Raje

राज्य मंत्री (स्वतंत्र प्रभार)
लघु उद्योग और कृषि एवं ग्रामीण उद्योग मंत्रालय
भारत

Minister of State (independent charge)
Ministry of Small Scale Industries
and Agro and Rural Industries
India

October, 1999.

Dear Shri Ravindranath

Thank you very much for your kind greetings on my success in the recent Lok Sabha Elections and induction into Cabinet. I greatly value the sentiments expressed by you.

I hope you will continue to extend your cooperation in helping me fulfil my responsibilities.

Yours sincerely,

(VASUNDHARA RAJE)

Shri C.V. Ravindranath
Managing Partner
Kunhikannan
Jewellery Gold House
Cannanore - 670 001

6116/EAM/95

विदेश मंत्री
भारत
MINISTER OF EXTERNAL AFFAIRS
INDIA

October 21, 1999

Dear Shri C. V. Ravindranath,

Thank you for your letter of 9th October, and for your warm felicitations on the victory of the National Democratic Alliance in the elections. I do appreciate your having taken the trouble to write to me.

2. Thank you also for sending me a copy of the letter from the Foreign Minister of Canada addressed to you, on the need to combat international terrorism. Cross-border terrorism has become a scourge and India is committed to doing all it can to strengthen international cooperation to combat it effectively.

Yours sincerely,

[Jaswant Singh]

Shri C. V. Ravindranath,
Managing Partner,
Kunhikannan Jewellery Gold House,
Cannanore – 670 001.
Kerala.

प्रमोद महाजन
PRAMOD MAHAJAN

D.O.No.546/VIP/99

सूचना और प्रसारण मंत्री एवं
खाद्य प्रंसस्करण उद्योग मंत्रालय
नई दिल्ली- **110 001**
MINISTER OF
INFORMATION & BROADCASTING AND
FOOD PROCESSING INDUSTRIES
NEW DELHI-110 001

1 2 APR 1999

प्रिय राजगोपालजी

I have received your letter dated 21st February, 1999 alongwith a representation of Shri C.V. Ravindranath, Kannur, Kerala regarding non-telecast of any programme on DD1 & DD Metro on the night of 'Maha Sivarathri '.

I appreciate your deep concern on the matter. Necessary instructions are being issued for future on such occasions.

With regards,

Brotherly yours,

[PRAMOD MAHAJAN]

Shri O. Rajagopal,
Member of Parliament,
120 & 124, V.P.House,
Rafi Marg,
New Delhi - 110 0 01.

DEEPAK CHOPRA

निजी सचिव
गृह मंत्री
भारत
PRIVATE SECRETARY
HOME MINISTER
INDIA

December 30, 1998

Shri C.V. Ravindranath,
Managing Partner,
Kunhikannan Jewellery,
Gold House, Kannur – 670 001
KERALA

Sir,

I am desired to acknowledge receipt and thank you for your letter dated 24th December, 1998 and the enclosed letter from United Nations regarding International Terrorism. Hon'ble Home Minister has gone through it.

With best wishes,

Yours sincerely,

(DEEPAK CHOPRA)

राष्ट्रपति
भारत गणतंत्र
PRESIDENT
REPUBLIC OF INDIA

11 August, 1997

Dear Friend,

I thank you for your kind sentiments expressed on my assumption of office recently.

(K. R. NARAYANAN)

Shri C.V.Ravindranath
Managing Partner
Kunhikannan Jewellery
Gold House
Kannur
Kerala

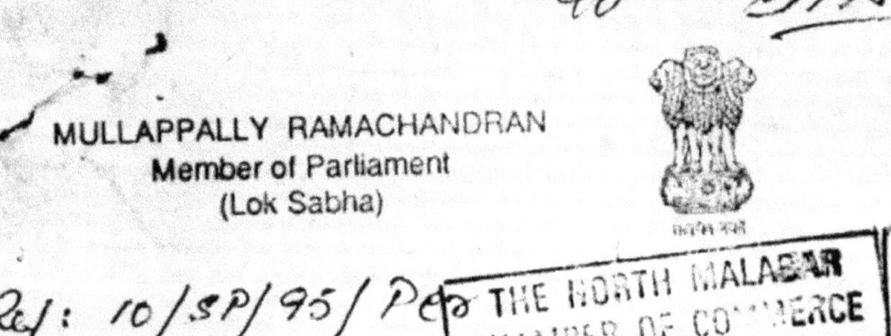

MULLAPPALLY RAMACHANDRAN
Member of Parliament
(Lok Sabha)

4, South Avenue Lane,
New Delhi-110011
Phone : 3017607

"Ravi" Post Chombala,
Calicut Dt. (Kerala)
Phones : 2345, 2222

Ref: 10/SP/95/P

THE NORTH MALABAR
CHAMBER OF COMMERCE

6 JUN 1995

CANNANORE-670 002.

29-05-'95

Dear Sir,

I have your letter regarding Indian Institute of Management in Kerala.

I have already taken up the matter with the concerned authorities and shall let you know after hearing from the minister.

With regards.

Yours sincerely,

Mullappally Ramachandran

Sri. C.V. Raveendranath,
Hon. Secretary,
North Malabar Chamber of Commerce,
Canannore- 670 002.

N. K. KUMARAN
MEMBER
KERALA LEGISLATIVE ASSEMBLY

CAMP: Cannanore

DATE 12/6/72

Conduct Certificate

This is to Certify that Shri C. V. Raveendran S/o Shri Chandukutty of Thavakkara, Cannanore is known to me for the last Ten years In fact he is well behaved youth bearing an exemplary conduct & Character

N. K. Kumaran
1/6/72

N. K. KUMARAN
CHAIRMAN
MUNICIPAL COUNCIL
CANNANORE.

PRAYER TO GODDESS SARASWATI

Oh! Goddess of knowledge, Saraswati, the giver of boons, the embodiment of fulfilling all my wishes, my salutations unto you. I begin my education with thy blessings and may there always be accomplishments for me.

സത്യം * ജ്ഞാനം * ധർമ്മം * കർമ്മം * അർത്ഥം
KISNA